Jogging with
G. K. Chesterton

65
Earthshaking
Expeditions

by Robert Moore-Jumonville

Introduction by Dale Ahlquist   Illustrated by Brian Shaw

JOGGING WITH G.K. CHESTERTON:
65 EARTHSHAKING EXPEDITIONS

Copyright © 2014 Robert Moore-Jumonville

Winged Lion Press
Hamden, CT

Winged Lion Press titles may be purchased for business or promotional use or special sales.

10-9-8-7-6-5-4-3-2-1

WINGED LION PRESS

ISBN 13   978-1-935688-07-5

To Kimberly Moore-Jumonville,
love of my life and my chief running partner,
whom I continue to chase after all these years.

CONTENTS

JOGGING WITH G.K. CHESTERTON

FOREWORD

The last time that I ran five miles. . . well, I have never run five miles. Maybe five miles total in my whole life.

Robert Moore-Jumonville says that he probably would have had a hard time convincing G.K. Chesterton to go jogging with him. I tend to agree with that conclusion, even though he is unsure of it himself. The evidence is not that Chesterton weighed three hundred pounds. I'm sure there are lots of three hundred pound joggers – or at least lots of joggers who if you put them together, would add up to three hundred pounds. No, the only reason I believe Robert could not have convinced Chesterton to go jogging with him is that he has never convinced *me* to go jogging with him. And he has tried. He tries every time he sees me. Which is only about once a year. Though I wish it were more frequent. Because I'm fond of saying "no" to him.

But there was one notable time when I did not say "no" to him. It was when he came to me with an idea for a column in a magazine that I publish, a magazine devoted to the aforementioned Chesterton. The column would be called "Jogging with G.K." Now you may think that I said "yes" simply because I must be hard up for material because I'm stuck with a magazine that is stuck on only one writer. You would be wrong. A magazine about G.K. Chesterton is a magazine about everything because Chesterton wrote about everything. And he wrote a lot about everything. And everything else. We have published the magazine for seventeen years. We have never run out of material, and we never *will* run out of material. But will we ever *run*? Not I.

And yes, I thought his idea for the column was crazy. But then, I already thought that Robert was crazy for being a jogger. However, the juxtaposition of "jogging" and "G.K." is a paradox worthy of Chesterton himself, a combination of two facts that seem to contradict one another.

I thought of Chesterton, who once spent a weekend visiting his friend, H.G. Wells, and said to him, "We are not going to have to go on any walks, are we?" I thought of the time when Chesterton could not get out a cab, and the driver said, "Perhaps if you try to get out sideways, Mr. Chesterton. . ." and the giant replied, "I have no sideways." I thought of his later days, living in the small village of Beaconsfield, west of London, when he and his wife Frances would occasionally hire a car to go on an evening drive, "for exercise."

Jogging with G.K.? Impossible! But perfect!

Robert wrote the column for us for twelve years. I learned a few things from him during that time, because, after all, that's how long it takes to graduate from high school. I learned, for instance, to become an ocular athlete. If you don't know what that is, I suggest you read this book. I also suggest you strive to become an ocular athlete, too.

I am grateful that his columns have become a book. It is of course a great pleasure to see more and more books about G.K. Chesterton popping up. And when I say "popping up," I mean that each of the new books has something surprising about it: Chesterton as a Philosopher, Chesterton as a Theologian, Chesterton as the spiritual and intellectual heir to Cardinal Newman, Chesterton as a Mystic, even Chesterton as a Saint. But surely none will raise as many eyebrows as Chesterton as a Jogger.

But wait, didn't we just establish that Chesterton is not a jogger, due to his great size, and due to the fact that, well, he's been dead for over 75 years? Well, even though Robert could probably not convince Chesterton to go jogging with him, the fact is Robert *does* jog with G.K. He reads and absorbs him and then reflects on him as he runs. He sees the world through Chesterton's eyes, filled with wonder. He sees meaning in everything and that nothing is insignificant. He thinks Chesterton's great thoughts along with him. And the greatest of the great thoughts is thanks. "Thanks," says Chesterton, "is the highest form of thought." We can only approach the gift of existence with gratitude. Chesterton talks about being thankful for the presents you find in your Christmas stockings on Christmas mornings, but that the best present you can ever find in your stockings is your own two legs. Certainly a jogger appreciates that idea, perhaps even more than the rest of us.

And even greater than the gift of existence is the gift of redemption, a thing we deserve even less and so must appreciate even more. It is the depth and height of grace. Even the length of grace, the next mile of it. Always worth meditating on. Meditation does not have to be taken sitting down. Meditation is itself an active engagement with divine truth. It is not passive. Robert understands this every time he goes on one of his <u>running meditations.</u>

Lace up your jogging shoes and join him. But in your case, you don't even have to get out of your chair.

Dale Ahlquist

President, American Chesterton Society

Jogging With G.K. Chesterton

PREFACE

G. K. Chesterton remains one of the most quoted and quotable writers in the English language. While his prose strikes readers as clever, it almost always contains a deeper meaning, revealing a spiritual perception of the universe and of the place human beings occupy in the world. Chesterton's vision of life—what I'd call his implicit "spiritual theology"—communicates clarity, wholeness, meaning, and sanity. For over twenty years Chesterton has served as my intellectual and spiritual mentor. His zest for life, love of people, and an ability to interpret life spiritually ground the essays in my book.

Those who know Chesterton best have taught me that the superlative way to introduce the man is through his own words. Chesterton began his book *All Things Considered* with a chapter entitled *The Case for the Ephemeral*, defending what he knew some might regard as a random collection of essays. I can think of no better introduction of and defense for my own collection of essays than the following words from Chesterton. In his preface, he commiserates with his readers:

> I cannot understand the people who take literature seriously; but I can love them, and I do. Out of my love I warn them to keep clear of this book. It is a collection of crude and shapeless papers upon current or rather flying subjects; and they must be published pretty much as they stand. They were written, as a rule, at the last moment; they were handed in the moment before it was too late, and I do not think that our commonwealth would have been shaken to its foundations if they had been handed in the moment after. They must go out now, with all their imperfections on their head, or rather on mine; for their vices are too vital to be improved with a blue pencil, or with anything I can think of, except dynamite.
>
> Their chief vice is that so many of them are very serious; because I had no time to make them flippant. It is so easy to be solemn; it is so hard to be frivolous. Let any honest reader shut his eyes for a few moments, and approaching the secret tribunal of his

soul, ask himself whether he would really rather be asked in the next two hours to write the front page of the *Times*, which is full of long leading articles, or the front page of *Tit-Bits*, which is full of short jokes. If the reader is the fine conscientious fellow I take him for, he will at once reply that he would rather on the spur of the moment write ten *Times* articles than one *Tit-Bits* joke. Responsibility, a heavy and cautious responsibility of speech, is the easiest thing in the world; anybody can do it. That is why so many tired, elderly, and wealthy men go in for politics. They are responsible, because they have not the strength of mind left to be irresponsible. It is more dignified to sit still than to dance the Barn Dance. It is also easier. So in these easy pages I keep myself on the whole on the level of the *Times*: it is only occasionally that I leap upwards almost to the level of *Tit-Bits*.

I resume the defense of this indefensible book. These articles have another disadvantage arising from the scurry in which they were written; they are too long-winded and elaborate. One of the great disadvantages of hurry is that it takes such a long time. If I have to start for High-gate this day, I may perhaps go the shortest way. If I have to start this minute, I shall almost certainly go the longest. In these essays (as I read them over) I feel frightfully annoyed with myself for not getting to the point more quickly; but I had not enough leisure to be quick.

Everything Chesterton confesses here to his readers, I too admit regarding my book. And though I have several fine people to thank for reading my manuscript and giving me advice and encouragement along the way, none of them can be blamed for the result.

Chesterton has served as inspiration throughout this project in a number of ways. First, together with Chesterton, if I have in any way succeeded at becoming an author, it is because I first failed to become an artist (art being the subject I majored in my first semester of college). More significantly, I took Chesterton's advice for young journalists quite seriously when in his *Autobiography* he suggested: "I have a notion that the real advice I could give to a young journalist is simply this: to write an article for the Sporting Times and one for the Church Times and put them in the wrong envelopes . . ." In Chesterton's estimate, the result would be that the readership of each paper would consider the off-topic article as a flash of brilliance. *Jogging With G. K. Chesterton* was written over a thirteen-year period as a regular column appearing in *Gilbert Magazine*, the publication of the American Chesterton Society. At the outset I had to consider what topic I knew enough about for a regular column and it was then that Chesterton's advice came to mind. Though I played soccer in high school and college, after seminary the leagues in my area played games on Sundays. As a new pastor working on a Ph.D., I needed a form of exercise that provided stress relief and took the least amount of time from start to finish. Running it would have to be. I've used the word "jogging" in the column and book not only because it alliterates better with G.K. but also because "running" might give the impression that I care about speed or that I've ever run competitively. Nothing could be farther from the truth. If anything, I've learned from Chesterton to run more slowly. In that sense, one of the recurrent themes of these essays calls us to pay attention, to notice what is, so that we might better appreciate and enjoy the life we already are living.

Since the start of my jogging career in 1987 (mainly occurring in the Midwest) I've always tried to keep Chesterton's writing as central to the essays, but I've interwoven his ideas with my own experience on the trail: experiences of creation, elements of culture, and my growing understanding of spirituality. I have grouped the essays according to subtopics instead of the order in which they were written, intending the reader to be able to pick the book up anywhere and read essays separately (as meditations) according to what seems to fit the current mood or moment.

I come now to the happy point where I get to thank all those who contributed to my little project. Instead of trying to sort out importance of influence, I'll jog through my offerings of gratitude here chronologically.

My first thanks and deepest appreciation goes to my adorable mate Kimberly—for a number of reasons. When Kimberly and I married in 1982 she did not jog so I ran my first years without her. But a couple of years later, when we found ourselves in rural Illinois, she bravely began to run with me. When our daughter, Annesley, was born in 1996 she too became part of our routine (by that time in Indiana), encountering her early view of the world from a jog stroller. Kimberly still joins me on the first leg of most of my runs (we do four miles together). She and I have run for over twenty-five years, logging approximately half of my 30,000 miles alongside me. At a slow pace, 15,000 miles has given us countless hours to process our lives verbally—to plan, problem-solve, laugh, express our frustrations surrounding the workplace, hammer out personal misunderstandings, counsel one another spiritually, and declare to each other our unflagging devotion and love. Kimberly, in short, has been my partner in crime in everything expressed in this book. Moreover, as someone who teaches alongside me at Spring Arbor University (mainly in British Lit), she's also served as inspiration for particular articles, giving me ideas, or letting me work out my own ideas as we ran. And Kimberly has edited many of these pages over the years, saving me much embarrassment and the reader much suffering.

Taylor University (Upland, Indiana) became our home in the 1990s after Kimberly received a teaching position there. I pastored a small United Methodist Church, worked on my dissertation, and taught part-time at Taylor. During that period, David Neuhouser, a math professor at Taylor, invited Kimberly and me to participate in a team-taught course on C. S. Lewis and Friends. At the time, I had only read **Orthodoxy**, but David encouraged me to dive into Chesterton with both feet. I credit David with my subsequent immersion into the world of GKC. He also introduced me to **Gilbert** magazine. Thanks to all of our friends at Taylor's Center for the Study of C. S. Lewis and Friends; for their spirit of collaboration and for providing a venue where people can gather and engage in the delightful discussion of enchanting authors.

As mentioned earlier, these essays appeared first in **Gilbert**, the publication of the American Chesterton Society. My genuine gratitude goes out to chief editor, Sean Daily, for putting up with late submissions and missed deadlines, and to Therese Warmus the journal's literary editor who always cheered me on from the sidelines. None of the faults of the writing, however, can be laid at Therese's jogging trail, because her editorial efforts went directly to the printed articles and when I got around to preparing the manuscript for publication I relied on my originals.

Dale Ahlquist, author and president of the American Chesterton Society, has done more for the current Chesterton revival in our country than any other individual. All of us owe him a debt of deep appreciation. One valuable way to express that would be to send the American Chesterton Society our financial support. Somehow, Dale saw my proposal for a column visually (picturing Chesterton, the Giant Elf, in a sweat suit)—and was brave enough to give it a chance. He has been a good friend and encourager since we first met. Dale has spoken brilliantly several times at Spring Arbor University and has allowed me to speak frequently at Annual American Chesterton Society conferences. I continue to learn from Dale and gain inspiration from the example of his life and faith.

My brother, mentor, dear friend, and sometimes running partner,

Dr. Neil Jumonville, bought a subscription to *Gilbert* so he could share my writing. As so often in my life, he consistently encouraged the project. Family members Annesley Moore-Jumonville, Dr. Darrell Moore, Cameron More, and Sterling Moore; friends I've met at the Chesterton Society; and readers of *Gilbert* have offered welcome support over the years. Furthermore, my college and graduate students have allowed me to persecute them with as much Chesterton as I could shimmy into a class, providing valuable feedback as I've sought to understand Chesterton's spiritual theology. Another outstanding colleague at Spring Arbor University, Dr. Jack Baker, provided a last minute editing of parts of the book to sharpen the prose and save me from grammatical chagrin.

Finally, I want to thank Brian Shaw, chair of the art department at Spring Arbor University, for working with me on this project. Brian is a true collaborator and wonderful colleague, who exhibits the Chestertonian virtues of humility, humor, and graciousness. Brian finished his drawings at least two years ago, waiting patiently for me to wrap up my editing. When I began college as an art major I wanted to be able to do what Brian does in this book—to create art like his. God had other things in mind for me. I'm delighted, however, with Brian's illustrations. Writers often find it difficult to discern whether or not their ideas make sense. So when Brian read the manuscript a number of years ago and began producing the sketches depicted here, I felt incredible joy that he not only understood the heart of what I was saying, but that he could depict it so well. Brian's illustrations take Chesterton's ideas and mine to an entirely new creative level; his art, readers will agree, contributes an invaluable depth to the book—full of Chesterton's spirit of wonder and joy. Remember, Chesterton began as an artist; his own sketches are delightful.

Finally, though I've never convinced Dale Ahlquist to go running with me, I hold that out as an "eschatological hope"—that at least we'll do it one day together in the kingdom of heaven. And if currently you don't jog, consider starting tomorrow morning—perhaps as a form of prayer.

Robert Moore-Jumonville
Spring Arbor University
Easter, 2014

AND WHY ARE YOU DOING THAT?

I'm sure that if I had lived during Chesterton's lifetime, and had the extraordinary privilege of personally meeting him, it would be nearly impossible to convince him to go running with me—even if I had Belloc arguing on my side! Don't you think it's true that on plain principle G. K. would question the jogging/running phenomenon in our culture as just another narcissistic fad—along with vegetarianism, Tai Chi, and cosmetic surgery? Likely so. On the other hand, like other Englishmen and women of the early twentieth century, Chesterton was a walker, and for the British, this brand of walking is almost never merely a casual pastime. A walking tour could last well past a week and might stretch out for more than twelve miles a day. Perhaps by analogy, then, I could convince Chesterton that jogging today was justifiable: "Jogging in our culture is like what walking was in yours."

So why would anyone lace up a pair of running shoes, anyway, only to subject themselves to extreme weather, bodily pain, pathologically aggressive motorists, and (in August in the upper Midwest) insects nearly as big as Chesterton himself? Reasons could be multiplied but let's start with three: running benefits your health, it serves as a form of stress management (instead of kicking the couch or berating the family spaniel), and it offers an opportunity for us to practice an aesthetics of praise, whereby we experience God's creation at the pace he intended. Think of it—there may actually be individuals growing up in our society who will never know what a daisy or robin looks like because they have only seen it as a seventy-mile-an-hour blur.

In my case, I think I also could convince Chesterton that I had no other choice but to take up running. It all began in 1987, in rural Illinois. I should note at the outset that I had always despised running. For ten years of my life I had played soccer once or twice a day and considered any exercise that did not involve a ball and a goal as a form of athletic heresy or cowardice. But alas, I did not have enough time to play in a league. Standing a mere 5' 6", I needed some way to burn calories if I didn't want to be continually mistaken for an oversized beach ball. I also needed some form of stress-management. Running was the cheapest and most time-efficient—no team, no partner to schedule with, no travel time, no racquet club fees. Running would have do. "See, Gilbert, this makes sense so far, doesn't it? At least for me."

Then, after living for a spell in rural Illinois, a kind of slow miracle occurred. I discovered Melvin's field: a mile of winding, rolling cow pasture, with a meandering creek to jump, and three fences to climb, and pheasants and indigo buntings, and great horned owls and a muskrat, and once a red fox, and in the winter, ice on the splashing creek in layers of silver that would make a tapestry artist weep for joy. That route ran either four or six miles—one mile led through Melvin's field, the others stretched into a square configuration of gravel country roads. I've been running in the Midwest, in three different states now, for well over two decades. Dare I say it? God speaks to me through these fields and furrows. And God is teaching me a new language of prayer.

At the same time that I was rediscovering God's created order in the Midwest landscape and wildlife, I was discovering for the first time the writings of G. K. Chesterton. And as I began to converse with Chesterton about God, faith, beauty and other topics (often while on my run), he bequeathed to me a new language for interpreting the world around me—a language of gratitude, wonder, playfulness, and joy. So, I think that I might be able to plead with Chesterton, not only to recognize the logic of running, but to admit that there can be a kind of contemplative aesthetics of praise Christian runners experience.

Were Chesterton some how to be transported bodily in time to our day, I'd love to have the chance to invite him to go running together. I don't think he'd go for it. First, there would be the mundane logistical concerns to overcome—whether he could find running shoes to support his weight, what he should actually wear, and whether his body could stand the shock of a short jog. He might also be concerned to damage his reputation—he'd have appearances to keep up, after all. But with his indefatigable playfulness, I imagine G. K. might be tempted to go at least a few blocks. First, he'd notify the press and ask them to post several local warnings, declaring what time he intended to jog so that no one mistook the thunder and swaying for an earthquake. He'd call his lawyer and make sure that he would not be liable in any way for the wildlife that would flee the area or for water mains that might burst. In the end, I don't suppose we'd get very far before Chesterton would laugh so heartily at himself and the whole idea of himself jogging that he would end up on his back in the grass in rip-rollicking convulsions.

Others would soon join in.

Though I do think Chesterton could be persuaded both of the logic of jogging in our culture and the sheer theological joy of participating in God's creation through the act of jogging, I don't think he'd participate himself. I remember someone who said that although they couldn't teach universalism (the doctrine that all shall eventually be saved) as a teaching of the church, they could still hold on to it as an eschatological hope (that in the end, it just might be the way things turn out). In the same way, I'm holding out as an eschatological hope that one of my early tours of heaven might be in the form of jogging with G. K.

APOLOGIA PRO JOGGING WITH G.K.

Wasn't it Chesterton who asserted confidently, "I jog therefore I am"? Maybe not, but he was a jogger, you know. Don't you recall his poem, *The Strange Ascetic*, where he beamed: "Now he who runs can read it/ this riddle that I write/...But I, I cannot read it/ although I run and run"— stop right there! See Chesterton was a runner after all—he ran and ran.

"Not so fast," protests the reflective reader, "I can understand the connection between Chesterton and politics, or religion, but Chesterton and jogging? Isn't that stretching "The Man Who Was Sunday" a bit too far?"

Realistically, my only defense for this book is to appeal to Chesterton's own counsel for juvenile journalists. In his *Autobiography*, he confessed "I have a notion that the real advice I could give to a young journalist... is simply this: to write an article for the *Sporting Times* and another for the *Church Times*, and put them into the wrong envelopes." Chesterton's concern, here, is not necessarily with the subjects of sport (jogging) or the Church (religion). Instead, his point is two-fold—first, that meaning in life is manifold—that it is mediated through the ordinary life of sport as well as through the sacramental life of the Church. Second, Chesterton reminds us that sometimes it takes something as plain (or perhaps as vulgar) as a jogging shoe to wake us up to the meaning in front of us.

"All truth is God's truth." Everything one jogs past, therefore—a common garbage can or garage—conveys truth. I'm not sure if Chesterton ever cited this theological dictum from Saint Augustine's *On Christian Doctrine*, but he certainly preached it from his pen. "It is impossible for anything to signify nothing," he insisted. Or consider the well-known lines from a *Daily News* article [please excuse my insertions]:

> You cannot evade the issue of God, whether you talk about pigs or the binomial theory, you are still talking about Him. Now if Christianity be...a fragment of metaphysical nonsense invented by a few people, then, of course, defending it will simply mean talking that metaphysical nonsense over and over again. But if

Christianity should happen to be true...then defending it may mean talking about anything or everything [including jogging]. Things [along the jog] can be irrelevant to the proposition that Christianity is false, but nothing [along the jog] can be irrelevant to the proposition that Christianity is true.

Thus, to talk about anything—no matter how common—is to talk (at least implicitly) about God, in Whom all things live and jog and have their being.

But someone will ask why jogging? Why not judo or jam sandwiches? Good question. A jam sandwich might appear as a more suitable symbol for someone like Chesterton. Yet Chesterton insists that it does not matter whether you begin your argument with jogging or jump-ropes, with lamp-posts or ladders—in part because he affirms that truth and the source of truth do not contradict themselves. "In the case of this defense of the Christian conviction," he insists in *Orthodoxy*, "I confess that I would as soon begin the argument with one thing as another; I would begin it with a turnip or a taximeter cab." Turnips might serve Chesterton's purpose just as well as jogging. In fact, some of my friends accuse me of jogging about as fast as a turnip.

Often, Chesterton proposes a pillar box (a cylindrical British mailbox) in place of a turnip or lamppost as an example. The point is that each of these is a common contrivance. Chesterton leans, in fact, toward the most mundane object in view. For he understands that our civilization is comprised precisely of those things we take most for granted—growing crops, predictable postal service, sanitation, safely lighted streets at night, opportunity for an education, the freedom to jog where we choose. For G. K., all things human mysteriously evoke meaning. One is almost tempted to apply a description of Innocent Smith to Chesterton: "out of any homely and trivial object he could drag reels of exaggeration, like a conjuror."

G. K. offers an apologia (a defense) in *Tremendous Trifles* of what some readers might call a haphazard collection of essays. But he hopes the very randomness of topics will wake us up, when our eyes alight on "a bed-post or a lamp-post, a window blind or a wall"—perhaps like looking up from retying your shoe on a run and staring at seven motionless deer. What is it Chesterton hopes we will see when we glance at window or wall? He hopes we will begin to fathom first our existence, second our existence as a gift from God, and third how that existence is implied in even the simplest of entities we encounter daily. And if the common objects along our jog hold significance—tree and telephone pole—how much more should human relationships or the church's liturgy evoke awe in us?! In *The Weight of Glory* C. S. Lewis insists that we have never looked on a mere mortal. Everyone we encounter on a daily basis is in fact an immortal soul. We might suggest a parallel appeal from Chesterton: "You have never gone on a mere jog." Indeed, if all truth is God's truth, what better symbol than jogging to represent our human condition as an adventurous journey flying from home and back again?

THE TIME IT TAKES

"I am sick today, and therefore cannot run," claims one individual. Another confesses she is so out of shape that running would make her sick. A third person declares, "My exercise comes from playing racquetball." Admittedly, reasonable excuses for *not* running exist.

The one excuse, however, which must not be taken seriously, is in fact the one most used: "I don't have enough time," or "I'm too busy." I do not want to appear unsympathetic. I know we're all busy—often with legitimate busyness, like trying to feed our families. Moreover, each year I grow older, my pace slows down, extending the time it takes me to run. And since we seem to believe "time is money," we imagine running is a waste of time. It's as if we think that only those things that create a profit possess value. Yet, as Wayne Muller points out, oil tanker spills, airplane crashes, terrorist attacks, wars, and catastrophic health crises all boost GDP (Gross Domestic Product). Then he asks:

> How do we count friendship or laughter? How do we count the value of honesty, or bread from an oven? How can we count the sunrise, the trusting clasp of a child's hand, a melody, a tear, a lover's touch? So many precious things grow only in the soil of time, and we can only begin to know their value when we stop counting.

Relationships grow only in time. Think how much time it takes to make a meal from scratch rather than succumbing to a dinner of processed and pre-packaged pellets (the ingredients of which remain a mystery). Then imagine what happens when we create a meal in our kitchen with family or friends. Time invested well often puts us in touch with other people; and always it connects us to our "place" in the world (in this case, a kitchen and dining room).

Ironically, we have sped up certain aspects of our lives in the hope of gaining more time. Fast food, fast cars, fast phones. But is our fast food really food? Our cars promised to get us places faster but we find ourselves stuck in traffic. In his essay *The Relics of Medievalism* Chesterton considers the complaint that road tolls are slowing down automobiles. "Is it indeed so certain," he asks, "that, if we can only make every sort of motor go faster and faster, we shall all be saved at last?" He avers that the "truly modern philosophy" has made motors more important than men.

The same holds true for the telephone, suggests Chesterton. The man who actually took the time to appreciate the wonder of the telephone—"bowing three times as he approached the shrine of the disembodied oracle," expressing his amazement and wonder to the operator who connects him to 666 Upper Tooting—"would, in fact, be in practice an opponent of all he desired to uphold," worse than any Luddite machine smasher. For that man would be taking too much time. As the recent AT&T ad demonstrates, our young children are learning that "faster is better." Our smart phones promised to make our work and our communication more efficient but we realize instead that we can no longer leave work at the office.

Chesterton foresaw our harried lives once in a nightmarish dream. He found himself

> Sitting at lunch in one of those quick-lunch restaurants in the City where men take their food so fast that it has none of the quality of food, and take their half-hour vacation so fast that it has none of the qualities of leisure. To hurry through one's leisure is the most unbusiness-like of actions. They all wore shiny hats as if they could not lose an instant even to hang them on a peg. And they all had one eye a little off, hypnotized by the huge eye of the clock. In short, they were slaves of the modern bondage, you could hear their fetters clanking. Each was, in fact, bound by a chain; the heaviest chain ever tied to a man—it is called a watch-chain.

We find ourselves tyrannized by a frenzied clock. Inglewood admits he's drugging himself with speed: "Pedaling the machine so fast that I turn into a machine." Most of us suffer from hurry sickness. We cannot run because we are running too fast. "Too busy to wake up," observes Inglewood. And then something strikes him: "There must be something to wake up to.... We're always preparing for something—for something that never comes off." The faster we go the more we have to do.

So my question is *why* don't we take time to run. Our excuse is that running is not efficient. We have too much to do. But judging on the basis of efficiency only makes us pedal faster. As Chesterton says, "it is futile because it only deals with actions after they have been performed.

It has no philosophy for incidents before they happen; therefore it has no power of choice."

Shouldn't we be asking, first of all, what the well-lived human life looks like? Only then can we move on to the subsidiary matter of the time it takes to achieve that life. Consider running as an invitation to join the human race.

RIDDLES ON THE RUN

I was running with Rodge, a friend who is unfamiliar with Chesterton (well, he actually knew a few lines of Chesterton without recognizing their source). So when on mile two of eight he began asking about Chesterton I took it as an opportunity for evangelism. Rodge demands: "How would you define Chesterton's literary career? I mean, was he an apologist, a novelist, or what?" At the pace we were running, I knew I had a captive audience for at least another fifty minutes. And what a great question! How *does* one categorize the essence of Chesterton's literary legacy? I remember looking through the combined contents of the *Chesterton Review* once and noticing all the "Chesterton as" articles— you know, "Chesterton as Theologian," "Chesterton as Literary Critic," "Chesterton as Poet," and so on. The fact is Chesterton was all of these things—and more. He was an artist, a biographer, a poet, a historian, a theologian, and all the while a churchman. Just glance through any one of the volumes of the *Illustrated London News* and try to fathom the wide variety of subjects G. K. tackles.

As I'm quickly preparing my answer for Rodge, Chesterton's designation of himself as a journalist in his *Autobiography* also flits through my mind. (But can Chesterton devotees ever be satisfied with that appellation as anything other than a prime example of Chesterton's self-deprecating humility?). It seems that while all these labels for G.K. are feasible there must be a broader category under which at least most of them could be subsumed—not just as some hyper-semantic exercise to tidy up the thought of a genius—but as a way of accurately disclosing the breadth of Chesterton's brilliance.

We were in the deep-cold Michigan winter on this particular run, which meant our gasping conversation would be muted through layers of baklavas and ski hats. "Man of letters comes to mind as perhaps an apt term for Chesterton," I muffled to Rodge as the frozen north shoreline of Lime Lake came into view: "Man of letters as in the general criticism of men like Matthew Arnold, John Ruskin, or Thomas Carlyle—thinkers who mainly employed the essay as a means of addressing the cultural crises of their day, and who appealed not primarily to an elite coterie of scholars, but to the public at large. Like Chesterton, these men wrote on every conceivable topic related to the health or sickness of their society." I was delighted when Rodge indicated interest in the direction of our conversation. I continued with a caveat: "There are enough differences, however, between Chesterton and these Victorians to warrant coining a particular phrase for Chesterton. The one I like is "cultural critic," or even better "Christian cultural critic."

Met now with silence except for the shush of an icy wind as we turned north and the rhythmic crunching of our shoes on the roadside snow, I knew I needed to elaborate on a few of the distinguishing features of what I meant by cultural critic. The first, I said, might be described as a commitment to transform one's culture through ideas—through ideas directed toward the average educated person by means of ordinary or popular methods of communication. So Chesterton wrote in a compelling style that would draw readers to his message and he used every genre imaginable. A cultural critic today might write for such publications as *First Things, Books and Culture, Touchstone, Atlantic Monthly*, or even the local paper to get his or her message out. Chesterton trusted that the common person could understand important ideas.

Second, Chesterton was an intellectual, perhaps the most significant aspect of cultural criticism. In contrast to the academician or scholar who is supposed to be neutral and objective, by definition an intellectual is impassioned and polemical. He or she cares about the topic at hand and defends it tooth and nail.

By the time I had communicated all this, we were on our last mile, but surprisingly, although Rodge agreed this was a worthy task to undertake in the British milieu a century ago, he was unclear that in our fragmented, postmodern culture such an exchange of popular, yet intellectual ideas was possible. That's how the conversation ended. Since then, I've thought of several responses that I'd like to offer my skeptical friend. First, I think I'll email him the quote where G. K. advises would-be-journalists to write two articles, one on religion and one on sports, and send them (as if by mistake) to the wrong presses. In other words, the sheer novelty of the cultural critic's ability to cross the boundaries fenced off by specialists may entice an open readership. Second, I think I should send Rodge a gift subscription to *Gilbert Magazine*.

A Crazy Thing to Do

The president of the American Chesterton Society, Dale Ahlquist, once confided in me that he had always believed joggers were an insane lot, but that he was rethinking this view after meeting several joggers he liked. Now, Dale's intuitions are often keen and should never be taken lightly. In fact, all joggers *are* mad, but they are not all mad in the same way. There are runners, of course, who are as mad with their running as mad mathematicians are with their numbers (mad as hatters). For instance, a colleague of mine insists his running is the only thing in his life that is measurable and he counts every mile he runs every year. This year he is already up to 327 miles, with a lifetime total of 43,721 miles. Now, in itself, there is nothing particularly insane about measuring, unless or until it becomes a kind of neurosis where the broad, beautiful world of snow-bedazzled fields and furrows, low-flying hawks, and Wordsworthian meadows is suddenly reduced to the measure of an odometer. Recall in *Orthodoxy* where Chesterton suggests the madman's mind "moves in a perfect but narrow circle." He shrinks his universe to fit into his brain, and it is his brain that bursts.

Another form of runner's madness is evident in the kind of fundamentalism where every person one meets becomes a target for conversion. Not only must you take up running; but you must also follow my "denomination's" rules of running. There can be no room for ecumenical discussion with this kind of jogger. Brand of shoe, distance and routine of run, carb intake—these are all written somewhere on Gortex tablets. There is something very puritanical about this approach to running that would have made G. K. cringe.

But there is another kind of running madness that is more like spiritual ecstasy, more like Chesterton's daily wonderment at the world. Don't get me wrong: the joy that comes from running is not to be confused with the kind of pleasure one gets from eating, say, a bacon-lettuce-tomato sandwich on toasted wheat in a sidewalk café on a sunny Toronto day. Running is hard work. It's often a chore; even a spiritual battle at times. In Paul's words, "I do not do what I want." Let's just say there is an ascetical element in running, an element of voluntary pain, or self-deprivation that is akin to fasting. But just as Paul compares his spiritual battle with that of an athlete, declaring, "I punish my body and enslave it" (1 Corinthians 9:27), you could as easily announce that running has the potential to be an ally for us in the spiritual life. Saint Francis is, I think, our model in this regard. Listen to how Chesterton describes the asceticism of Francis as a kind of activism:

> There was nothing negative about it; it was not a regimen or a stoical simplicity of life. It was not self-denial merely in the sense of self-control. It was as positive as a passion; it had all the air of being as positive as a pleasure. He *devoured* fasting as a man devours food. He *plunged* after poverty as men have dug *madly* for gold (italics added).

Chesterton describes for us here one of the foundational principles of spiritual formation—that less can mean more. Eat less food, practice fasting, and suddenly you are shocked by the joy of the simplest sustenance. In an apple one finds a feast, in a handful of raisins a miracle.

The madness of runners, then, when at its best, becomes much more than merely an endorphin-charged euphoria. Spiritually, the runner briefly tastes—almost as a symbol to be interpreted—the simplicity, solitude, and inner freedom found by Saint Francis. For the solitary runner, there is a detachment from people, schedules, and things, and in turn, an embracing of all creation as a precious gift. All becomes gift: weather, earth, creatures, legs, sight, and breath. We deserve none of these. We can only respond with wonder and gratitude. "For there is no way in which a man can earn a star or deserve a sunset," Chesterton reminds us. "It was by this deliberate idea of starting from zero... that [Saint Francis] did come to enjoy even earthly things as few people have enjoyed them." Starting out on the run, then, with nothing but the clothes on her back, the runner receives in return a hundred-fold: sunsets, swans on glistening ponds, and deer that leap fences like a ballet team. I sometimes think that the woods I run through are much more "mine," in one sense, than their owners', because I know these fields, oaks, and brambles, whereas their owners do not even know they exist. And I don't have to pay the taxes! In the last analysis, the madness of the runner is like the madness of Chesterton's grateful "man alive." Maybe that's what intrigues Dale about runners.

RUNNING SUICIDE

"Running is suicide," my friend unquestioningly remarked. "Or perhaps, for some, 'not running' is suicide?" I retorted. Chesterton has helped me develop my theology of suicide.

As a young man we know Gilbert teetered on the brink of suicide. Some would suggest it was merely the "suicide of thought" he contemplated. "I listened with a sort of calm horror of detachment, suspecting that there was nothing but mind," he recalled in his *Autobiography*. Gary Wills, in his rendering of this period of Chesterton's life, emphasizes the intellectual crisis: "This was the solipsist's threat, the 'critical problem' which haunts the post-Kantian world.... subjectivity carried to a logically complete and paralyzing subjectivism...." However, perhaps Chesterton's crisis was more serious, such that he contemplated physical suicide. In the *Autobiography* he only suggests that he plunged deeper and deeper into his despairing nightmare "as in a blind spiritual suicide." He confided in a letter to his closest friend, Edmund Bentley that he descended "very far into the abysses, indeed...."

In fact, much of Chesterton's early work demonstrates an intimate preoccupation with the topic of suicide, often paralleling it with non-existence. Recall, for instance, the important contrast he makes between the martyr and the suicide in *Orthodoxy*. Examples of Chesterton's fascination with non-existence could be piled high. For instance, one of the important poems in *The Wild Knight and Other Poems*—Gilbert's second publication (1900)—*Thou Shalt Not Kill*, suggests how personal this topic was for Chesterton. The reader is tricked into thinking that the narrator is contemplating killing some enemy perhaps: "I had grown weary of him." Then the last stanza performs a somersault:

> Then I cast down the knife upon the ground
> And saw that mean man for one moment crowned
> I turned and laughed: for there was no one by—
> The man that I had sought to slay was I.

What we read in *The Wild Knight and Other Poems*, however, does not breed despair in the long run, but instead trumps nihilism with a Christian confidence in human dignity and value fashioned after the image of God.

A Ballade of Suicide, appearing later in *Poems*, beautifully represents Chesterton's paschal intuition that out of the winter-death threat of non-existence blooms an appreciation for the simplest facts of every day life—the sorts of things encountered on one's morning run. The narrator's whimsical depiction of the spiffy gallows in his garden and the line of neighbors arrayed along the wall to watch him hang himself contrasts with the poem's refrain: "I think I will not hang myself today." One could say the poem smirks with a tongue-in-cheek attitude, not so much to exorcise past fears as to spotlight present Innocent-Smith-like appreciation. The second stanza is worth deliberation:

> To-morrow is the time I get my pay—
> My uncle's sword is hanging in the hall—
> I see a little cloud all pink and grey—
> Perhaps the Rector's mother will *not* call—
> I fancy that I heard from Mr. Gall
> That mushrooms could be cooked another way—
> I never read the works of Juvenal—
> I think I will not hang myself to-day.

Notice, first, how almost anything justifies continuing existence. The day may not turn out as badly as we thought—perhaps the Rector's mother will *not* drop by. But even marveling at mundane cloud formations, or relishing the flavor of a new recipe, might warrant staying alive at least another day. His uncle's sword hanging in the hall conjures up images of the childlike antics of Innocent Smith, in *Manalive*: just imagine what games one could invent with a sword! And the works of Juvenal—an obscure Roman satirist and poet—may prove enjoyable: who can know without trying. Perhaps we would read Juvenal aloud to one another until we pealed with side-splitting laughter. Who knows if the run this morning would turn out gloriously—the weather, the scenery, maybe I will have energy I didn't count on—who knows, unless we give it a try?

In *Orthodoxy*, Chesterton clearly connects the precarious human condition—"that any man in the street is a Great Might-Not-Have-Been"—with a deep appreciation for the simple things that *are*. All objects pulled from Crusoe's sinking ship on to the solitary island would be appreciated. "But it is a better exercise still to remember how all things have had this hair-breath escape: everything has been saved from a wreck." Any run then perhaps counts as a Great-Might-Not-Have-Run!

In a way, running can symbolize for our sedentary culture Innocent Smith's pistol shot through the hat of modern man—a wake up call, as it were, announcing both the reality of human finitude and the gift of tangible life: that "in some way all good [is] a remnant to be stored and held sacred...." All is gift, all is good, all is God. As Chesterton confessed: "when the heavens were compared to the terrible crystal I can remember a shudder. I was afraid that God would drop the cosmos with a crash."

But it is the last line of *A Ballade of Suicide* that I most frequently repeat on my run: "And through thick woods one finds a stream astray,/ so silent that the very sky seems small." And I can't help but add my own ending these days: "I think I will not skip my run today."

FEAR OF OUR GOODNESS

"One of these days I plan on starting a running regimen," my overweight friend insists; "but for now I'm still working on carbo-loading." Certainly, Chesterton would have appreciated this remark for its candor and wit. But I imagine Chesterton also surveying our culture's flippancy and commenting: "Impartiality is a pompous name for indifference." An off-the-cuff attitude can lead toward apathy, or toward spiritual deterioration, for as Chesterton cautioned, reform requires constant vigilance; how much more so, renewal of the human heart? Orthodoxy has "always maintained that men are naturally backsliders," said Chesterton; "that human virtue tended of its own nature to rust or rot." C. S. Lewis summed up our spiritual condition by suggesting that through the daily choices we make, we are slowly becoming either a more hellish or more heavenly creature. I'm reminded of the analogy William James used in his essay *The Will to Believe*: if you are on a mountain pass when a blinding blizzard strikes, going forward on the path means the risk of sliding over a precipice; but to stand still means potentially freezing to death. Not to choose also implies a choice. Apathetically refusing to choose still constitutes choosing.

But our indifference is fostered by fear. We fear committing to a spiritual workout because we suppose we cannot match up. We fear running because we're not sure we'll finish the race. Our culture gives up in advance, settling for the mundane. It's the spirit of the age sketched by the Notting Hill narrator: that "vague and somewhat depressed reliance upon things happening as they have always happened, which … had become an assumed condition. There was really no reason for any man doing anything but the thing he had done the day before." So fear produces reluctance, reluctance degenerates into the deadly sin of sloth, and sloth whispers just the right excuses for me not to run. Is it our weakness that frightens us most? Is it the fact that we know too well our human condition as fallen, sinful creatures; is that what holds us back from becoming who we were made to be in Christ—a little less than the angels?

"The true doctrine of original sin may be stated in a million ways, like every very central and solid truth. You may put it this way: that moral health is not a thing which will fulfill itself automatically in any complete man like physical health. Or this way: that we all start in a state of war. Or this way: that everything in a cabbage is trying to make a good cabbage, whereas everything in a man is not trying to make what we call a good man."

We know our own weakness and fallen state if we're honest, though I do not mean all people should be runners. I only refer to those of us who decide to run, who really want to run, but who then don't do the very thing they want to do (as Romans chapter 7 might phrase it). It's not just that I disappoint my coach, boss, teacher, or family; I disappoint myself. When asked about the meaning of "the Fall," Chesterton answered, "That whatever I am, I am not myself." The mental recognition of this human dilemma can cause us to give up trying (or training) before we ever begin.

Consider, however, that another force may be at work in this process of fear and discouragement—one not often recognized—not the probability of our badness, but the very potential of our goodness. A student once commented in class that we fear our goodness more than our wickedness because if we admit our saintly capabilities we become responsible for them. Recently, I heard someone paraphrase Nelson Mandela as saying something similar: that human beings cannot bear the weight of their own inherent greatness. This is a dangerous business, warns Chesterton:

"The person who is really in revolt is the optimist, who generally lives and dies in a desperate and suicidal effort to persuade all the other people how good they are. It has been proved a hundred times over that if you really wish to engage people and make them angry, even unto death, the right way to do it is to tell them they are all sons of God."

The question is whether or not we are called to become saints, "sons of God" as Chesterton puts it. Because, if so, we might either give up the prospect in advance, or try some futile Pharisaical "program" for "self-salvation." Notice, however, in the Annunciation, that Mary ignores the worthiness question altogether, becoming, instead, a model of pure receptivity, fully open to divine grace. From a slightly different approach to assessing worthiness Pope Benedict XVI suggests that the Tax Collector who prays for mercy "draws life from being-in-relation" to

God, "receiving all as gift." He focuses on God's goodness, more than on his own wretchedness. Both the pure Mary and the tainted Taxman acknowledge a radical dependence on God. "The grace for which he prays does not dispense him from ethics," notes the Pope. "It is what makes him truly capable of doing good in the first place." The best arguments for running that I can discern for myself, therefore, would be as a better path to "being-in-relation" to God, or to receiving life as gift, or as a way of acknowledging my utter dependence on God.

JOGGING WITH G.K. CHESTERTON

A Circular Argument

For the sake of provoking a good argument in these pages—the kind Gilbert and Cecil would have relished—let me insist that there is no better symbol than the circle to represent the soul of Chesterton's thought.

Of course, Chesterton disliked the circle as a symbol. I am not thinking here of the traffic roundabouts that regularly suck innocent victims into an unending inescapable gyration—though surely with his directional dysfunction Gilbert had his run-ins with roundabouts. Nor is it merely that Chesterton found math tiresome, never asking "Y," causing algebraists to cry.

Instead, for Chesterton the circle symbolized a certain brand of insanity. Having lost everything except his reason, the modern materialist madman inhabits a tiny neat and tawdry round universe:

> Perhaps the nearest we can get to expressing it is to say...that [the mad man's] mind moves in a perfect but narrow circle. A small circle is quite as infinite as a large circle; but, though it is quite as infinite, it is not so large. In the same way the insane explanation is quite as complete as the sane one, but it is not so large.... There is such a thing as a narrow universality.

The sun into which we dare not stare represents mystery; the moon as a reasonable, observable circle "is the mother of lunatics." It might be sane to run on a small, circular indoor track, where the climate is perfectly controlled, and the shower lies down the hall, but if this were the only place one jogged, it would amount to a cramped, sterile—and in the end—inhuman running routine.

In another sense for Chesterton, the circle represents the rather lazy habit of allowing oneself to get mentally stuck in one place—as if a person only ever ran on a treadmill. Eastern yogis "have made many things out of [the circle], and sometimes gone mad about it, especially when ... the circle became a wheel going round and round in their heads."

But Eastern religion also employs the circle (or the wheel) more perilously, where mind and spirit close in upon themselves, like a strong hand crushing an orange:

> The mind of Asia can really be represented by a round 0, if not in the sense of a cypher at least of a circle. The great Asiatic symbol of a serpent with its tail in its mouth is really a very perfect image of a certain idea of unity and recurrence that does indeed belong to the Eastern philosophies and religions. It really is a curve that in one sense includes everything, and in another sense comes to nothing. In that sense it does confess, or rather boast, that all argument is an argument in a circle.

Similarly, the disc of the philosopher points to a circular argument, where everything begins and ends in the mind, shrinking finally into a stultifying solipsistic nightmare—into the nothing of non-existence.

On my morning run the other day, however, it struck me (half way around my "loop") that the circle might actually aptly signify a key aspect of Chesterton's thought. While most running routes, I suspect, consist of some sort of line pattern—an out-and-back configuration—even the turning around at the end suggests the arc of a circle.

It is this sort of circle (or perhaps more of an elliptical ring) that lies at the heart of his argument in *Orthodoxy*—which is "arranged," as he asserts, "upon the positive principle of a riddle and its answer." The riddle revolves around human nature—connected to human longing and fulfillment. "How can we contrive to be at once astonished at the world and yet at home in it?" he asks. Facetiously, the answer is to get off the couch and go jogging. That is one way to combine "something that is strange with something that is secure," to blend wonder and welcome. How enviable to adventure from home with the aim of discovering New South Wales, as the rash yachtsman in Chesterton's romance tale intended, only to realize "with a gush of happy tears that it was really old South Whales."

The circle of the run stands, therefore, for something deeply human—that desire "to have in the same few minutes all the fascinating terrors of going abroad combined with all the humane security of coming home again." And any out of door run evokes both trepidation and security if we're paying attention. It is impossible to run and not be astonished. Human beings cannot run impassibly (though perhaps zombies can).

At the end of Chesterton's argument in Orthodoxy it is really the Church that represents the return leg and destination point for the journey "home." Rather than the common caricature of the Church sketched among Western intellectuals as a joyless, barbaric, humorless legalism peddled by superstitious priests—from which we ought to flee in revulsion—the Church instead appears as living teacher leading us to our true home, as a secure playground full of dancing and delight. We inhabit a world of spirits, Chesterton maintains, populated with both good and evil spirits:

> So I shall search the land of void and vision until I find something like fresh water, and comforting like fire; until I find some place in eternity where I am literally at *home*. And there is only one such place to be found ... the Christian Church.

CONFESSIONS

One month I came close to not submitting an article to *Gilbert*, the magazine of the American Chesterton Society. I'm not sure how long I have had the privilege of persecuting people with this quirky column, with my mad Midwest meanderings about running. Over ten years, I'm guessing. I don't think I've skipped an article during that time (though missing the deadlines general editor Sean Dailey sets is another matter). Often in the past I've worked ahead, some summers writing the bulk of my articles for the coming year, after school finishes. But this one particular fall chaos descended thicker than the leaves and I "fell behind" in life. I realized if I did not submit a column, it might go completely unnoticed, which would be a proper humbling experience. Or the absence of my column might be heralded as an improvement for all sorts of good reasons: for one, it was in January and after so much holiday over-eating we often don't relish reminders of exercise.

I also realized good reasons exist for contributors not to offer an essay to a given publication. When we read through the *Illustrated London News*, for instance, we know there were periods and occasions when Chesterton, for all his prolific consistency, did not submit essays. From January 17 to May 22, 1920 Chesterton's columns were written by Hilaire Belloc and in the four-month period from February 12 to May 21 "J.D.S." replaced Chesterton as contributor. April 23, 1928 also reports no column for the week, and there are other gaps. Without scouring the detailed dates of Chesterton's biography we could deduce that during these absences he was either on holiday, or occasionally reporting in sick.

Then again, Chesterton may have absent-mindedly missed a deadline here and there. We could imagine many reasons for his pen remaining idle. Perhaps one day he woke up with a hangover and stayed in bed to draw; or maybe when the time came to deliver his completed essay, Chesterton found himself hopelessly lost—abducted by a strange cabman, wandering some unexplored plain in Brussels in the rain, or planted on the wrong train. When I asked my daughter, Annesley, what she thought might have kept G. K. Chesterton from submitting on a given day, she replied: "Maybe he burned his toast." Maybe. Or perhaps one day Gilbert's household was "unexpectedly invaded by infants of all shapes and sizes," as he relates in *The Real Journalist*. Of course, he immediately forgot about the article deadline and attended instead to arbitrating squabbles over who knocked down whose blocks, no doubt administering honorable verdicts among the warring children.

Just as he metes out principles of the highest morality,

> it occurs to him suddenly that he has not written his Saturday article; and that there is only about an hour to do it in. He wildly calls to somebody (probably the gardener) to telephone to someone for a messenger; he barricades himself in another room and tears his hair wondering what on earth he shall write about.

Absence of topic and lack of time create the dilemma: how to give the world a present of "fifteen hundred unimportant words."

Since, on short notice, I found myself needing to offer a present of approximately nine hundred extremely unimportant words, while also attempting to interject the topic of jogging; and let me suggest that, if there are good reasons not to write an essay, or meet a deadline, or go to work (on occasion), there also are jolly good reasons (at least every day one wakes up tired in the dead of Michigan winter) not to go running. I do realize discipline itself can count as a good thing. However, I also realize that for some folks running (apart from the necessity sometimes of running from danger—from mad dogs, fires, bad opera, etc.) is always an odious enterprise.

I take as an example an exchange that appeared on my Facebook page between Mike Foster and Miki Tracy (unknown to me until it mostly had played itself out). The discussion went like this: Foster: "running for fun is so NOT Chestertonian. Unless it was for last call @ Ye Old Cheddar Cheese." Tracy: "Running 'for fun' is unspeakably bizarre insanity. Personally, I'd rather stick myself in the eye with a fork whilst dancing a jig on a small slab of Styrofoam in the middle of the winter Pacific during an ice storm—now 'that' sounds like fun! Which is strange, because when I was eighteen, I could run two miles in twelve minutes on a humid July day....still didn't like it." Foster: "'Running for fun', even before I had anterior fractures of L1-3 vertebrae in 2000 & hip replacement three years ago, was an oxymoron. Michael Stipe of R.E.M. says it well: 'I'd rather chew my leg off.'"... The next 23 posts between these two zanies impersonate a George Burns-Gracie Allen comedy routine.

Sometimes I am dreadfully consistent at running (say five days out of seven), but like most things in my life, I get into slumps now and then. I wonder during the more brutal winter months if it's not mainly the wind. Not just the wind by itself. It's when I check the weather in the morning and notice not only that the temp is 20 degrees or lower, but that the wind is 15 mph or above. The excuse is begging to be used. And I ponder silently: "I think I will not hang myself today."

THE CONTEMPLATIVE RUNNER

Yesterday, I found it difficult to justify the time it takes to run—the time required to hydrate, dress, stretch, run, shower, and dress again for the day can take up to over two hours. My mind was crowded with more urgent things that needed doing. The lawn needed mowing; unopened emails stacked two feet deep stared at me from my computer monitor; colleagues called for meetings; for a week I had not spent any good time with my eight year old daughter; important things to do screamed at me from every corner: "Change the oil in your car," "Write your mother," "Catch up on the news," "Spend some time with your wife," "Finish your research project coming due." But I ran anyway.

On about mile four, with thoughts and worries still crowding in, competing with the cadenced crunching of the gravel road under my feet, a speeding pick up flew by in too much of a hurry for anybody's good. Why are we all in such a rush, I wondered? "Hurry is not of the devil," remarked Carl Jung; "it is the devil." Pascal declared, "I have discovered that all human evil comes from this, man's being unable to sit still in a room" (*Pense'* 139). When confronted with the sickness of his society, Kierkegaard prescribed silence:

> In observing the present state of affairs and of life in general, from a Christian point of view one would have to say: It is a disease. And if I were a physician and someone asked me 'What do you think should be done?' I would answer, 'Create silence, bring about silence.'

Chesterton offered a similar prognosis: "Wonder depends on some return to simplicity and even to slowness."

Yet when we try to quiet our minds and souls, thoughts and worries cascade down, urgently screaming for our attention. As one of the characters in Chesterton's *Manalive* moans, "We're too busy to wake up." That is why diversion is such an integral element of our culture. For as long as we are mildly distracted by some external stimulus—a good book or film (or bad ones, it mostly seems)—our thoughts lie low. Henri

Nouwen suggests that our thoughts are like chimpanzees in a banana tree: dance in front of the tree and the monkeys watch you fixedly, but try to meditate quietly under the tree and the chimps instantly explode into jumping and jabbering.

What we need, then, in our fast-paced culture are ways to disengage our minds without lobotomizing ourselves with cheap entertainment. We need some way to keep the monkeys quiet without expending our souls to entertain them ourselves. It sounds paradoxical, doesn't it? Is this possible—to take the car out of gear without totally shutting off the engine? Yet Chesterton understood the paradox perfectly: "There would be less bustle [in our epoch]," he recommended, "if there were more activity, if people were simply walking [or running] about. Our world would be more silent if it were more strenuous" (*Orthodoxy*).

This is where running enters the picture. God created us to live physically active lives. Like walking, or cross country skiing, or gardening, running can provide a person with just enough physical stimulus to set his or her mind at rest. C.S. Lewis used the example of a train ride. With the scenery going by, yet with nowhere to really go yourself, with nothing you really have to do, the mind is allowed to disengage and float freely in thought. The idea came from a friend of his who had once said:

> A railway compartment, if one has it to oneself, is an extremely good place to pray in 'because there is just the right amount of distraction.' When I asked him to explain, he said that perfect silence and solitude left one more open to the distractions which come from within, and that a moderate amount of external distraction was easier to cope with (*Letters to Malcom* 18).

The same can be true for runners. Something can happen while running which is very close to contemplative prayer, or to Brother Lawrence's "practicing the presence of God" where he converses easily with God elbow deep in dirty pots and pans. The goal of these kinds of prayer is to detach from thoughts that crowd into our consciousness, and instead, focus quietly on God's presence. Thomas Keating uses the image of junk floating down a river. When thoughts continue to tumble into our mind during contemplative prayer, we cannot help that. But we do not have to pluck the thoughts up and pull them out of the stream of consciousness, grasping them nervously. We can let them float by. We can wave to the junk as it drifts downstream and gently return our loving gaze upon God, our still center point.

Running can offer the perfect setting for this kind of letting go. No phones or computer. No Daytimer, Palm Pilot, I-Touch, or email. Nothing needs to be done in this next hour or so, because nothing can be done. Just let it go. As Peter Kreeft puts it: "Tiny things, like economics and technology and politics, no longer loom large, and enormous things, like religion and morality, no longer seem thin and far away" (*Christianity for Modern Pagans*). If, on the other hand, somewhere between mile four and eight, you hear a still small voice telling you to change your car oil or write your mother, let it go until the run is over; afterwards you will likely remember to do something about it.

THE SEER

"The traveler sees what he sees, the tourist sees what he has come to see," warns Chesterton. The Annual Conference of the American Chesterton Society is about learning to see. Of course, even those of us who attend the conference regularly don't know exactly what we're going to see— that is, what to expect. Yet every year, Chesterton veterans gather in August to see old friends—to see the world with a singular, sacramental joy, and to celebrate. Every year, new folks attend the conference hoping to see Chesterton more compellingly. They're never disappointed. And every year, we all gather, longing for Chesterton to lift the veil from our eyes so we can see Christ more clearly.

We know the aim of the American Chesterton Society Annual Conference is to open our eyes and wake us up, but our president, Dale, keeps us up so late, filling each day with so much that's good, that it's sometimes hard to stay awake. How can we take it all in—the book vendors' stalls, speakers, side conversations, special events and meals, and more—and still pack in a morning run?

We also know that one of the chief aims of Chesterton's writing is to help us see more clearly, so we don't bump through our lives as mere tourists. He wants us to notice the ordinary in front of us that we so easily take for granted; he wants to wake us to wonder so we recognize that every common object bears a sacramental stamp. In his Notebooks: Chesterton wrote: "A mystic is one who sees round every object/ A halo from a hidden sun."

But were we completely attentive on a good, long run, our head might split. Chesterton commented in the Daily News: "A person who never neglected any object: a man who burst into religious tears as he fastened a divine collar with an inspired collar-stud, and continued thus with everything he looked at, would go mad in five minutes; he would see God and die."

Naturally, the things we encounter every day on our morning run (since we become accustomed to them) are the things we most easily take for granted, and yet perhaps the very things we ought to be most grateful for: the stable earth beneath our feet, legs that move, clean air to breathe and water to drink, and a more or less clear mind. Indeed, Chesterton invites us to see the beauty and goodness of life in what is most ordinary.

In his Preface to *Tremendous Trifles*, he bellows: "Don't let us let the eye rest…. Let us exercise the eye until it learns to see the startling facts that run across the landscape as plain as a painted fence. Let us be ocular athletes. Let us learn to write essays on a stray cat or a colored cloud." I frequently see both colored cats and stray clouds on my running route, but how often I need Chesterton to remind me to see them, to notice and appreciate them. How often I fail to really see.

Standing in the middle of Battersea, Chesterton exclaimed to a friend:

> I cannot see any Battersea here; I cannot see any London or any England. I cannot see that door. I cannot see that chair: because a cloud of sleep and custom has come across my eyes. The only way to get back to them is to go somewhere else.

People ask me why I run, as if running were a form of self-flagellation. Perhaps the main reason I run is to wipe the cloud of sleep from my eyes so I notice the colored clouds.

Hugh Kenner calls Chesterton a contemplative: he wrote as he did, Kenner argues, because "his eyes were especially open." According to Kenner, "He sees more than other men see." In one of his books on Ignatian spirituality, David Fleming suggests that "our vision largely controls our perception," and also that, "right vision lies at the heart of our relationship with God." "Your eye is the lamp of your body," insists Jesus; "If your eye is healthy, your whole body is full of light, but if it is not healthy, your body is full of darkness" (Luke 11:34). Let's admit that we often miss the simple truth—saying we see, when in fact, we're still blind. Recall that the parables are spoken so that we might see, but not perceive—hear but not understand (Mark 4:12). Richard Rohr puts it this way: "How you see is what you see."

If you ask me what I see on my run, I could recite a list of objects— as Chesterton suggested that the best poetry consists of an inventory, like the items Crusoe pulled from his wrecked ship. But if I describe what I see on my run, then seeing ceases to be active—the verb of seeing turns into a set of nouns. Instead, Chesterton lived "seeing as an activity," as a form of prayer. The point of seeing lies in the seeing itself;

in the noticing—for only through greater attentiveness does wonder and appreciation grow.

A monk moved into town with his disciples. After a few months a delegation of townspeople came to him with a complaint: "All you and your disciples do is eat, and sleep, and go running!" "Ah," replied the monk, "but we know that we eat, and sleep, and go running."

HOARDING THE HILLS

When I run, I try to pay attention to my surroundings. That's partly why I run (jog) so slowly. When I began running in rural Illinois in 1987 as a form of stress release, I carried with me a pair of mini-binoculars and stopped frequently to identify owls, indigo buntings, mink, and other wildlife. Paying attention to our surroundings can serve as a way to acknowledge who God is and who we are and what he has done for us. It is a form of appreciation and gratitude; it is a way of saying, "Thank you, God, for this world." Chesterton stressed that we should encounter the world daily with a wonder and amazement capable of producing within us an invigorating gratefulness. "The aim of life is appreciation," said Chesterton, the goal is "to enjoy enjoyment," to register "astonishment at our own existence," "to remind [ourselves], by every electric shock to the intellect, that we are still [men] alive."

Most of us are familiar with the general lessons of praise that God's world teaches. The creation is magnificent. The psalmist blurts out: "When I look at your heavens, the work of your fingers, the moon and stars that you have established; what are human beings that you are mindful of them, mortals that you care for them?" Chesterton had the same kind of reaction when confronted with a dandelion (*Autobiography* 322). We go along on our route, keeping our schedule, eyes on the road ahead, when suddenly—wham!—the creation breaks in upon us and shakes us awake and amazes and astonishes us with its sheer beauty and wonder. That's God speaking, reminding us that an artist has been at work here. "The world is charged with the grandeur of God," declared Hopkins; "it will flame out like shinning from shook foil." Commenting on this verse in his journal, the poet observes, "All things are therefore charged with love, are charged with God, and if we know how to touch them, give off sparks and take fire, yield drops and flow, ring and tell of him." Everything in nature tells of God. "Make a joyful noise, all the earth." Yes, all the earth *is* raising a ringing, raucous praise; how can we keep silent? Even the rocks cry out. The trees of the fields clap their hands. Perhaps this is what Joseph Pieper meant by the "festive and paradise-evoking aspect of creation." The earth sings, the creek leaps and rolls, the birds all arrive wearing their finest, in honor of the coming king.

So, how come we so often miss it—the wonder of life? Children rarely miss a thing. You notice that children pay attention to everything. They value and esteem both the butterfly and the potato bug, both the daffodil and the dandelion. Take them to the zoo and children light up looking at ducks, squirrels, and sparrows on the sidewalks as much or more than watching the sleepy tiger and playful polar bears in their cages. Our Lord says: "Become more like these children: looking, listening, leaning into life." Chesterton even suggests the parallel between childlike energy and the playful nature of God who says to the sunrise each new morning: "Do it again!"

It behooves us to pay attention, too, because of what we are apt to miss if we do not. There are only certain days of the year that the ice paints every blade of grass individually, laboring all night to coat each twig and crumpled leaf and line of barbed wire fence by hand. There is only one day in two thousand you can witness the glory of the hedge-tree-dance in the fall. The day must be crisp-cold and perfectly still—not a waft of wind. And all the leaves fall at once; seemingly the whole tree defrocks in a matter of hours. And you can hear the flutter clearly, like a purr. Some butterflies are very seasonal—there are black ones with gorgeous cobalt blue wings, and rumor has it the monarchs are now endangered by some pesticide, so we had better pay attention while they are still with us.

When I can, I like to stretch out my hand to touch the grass on the side of the road as I run by. But then the town or county mowing crews roll along and cut it down, so I have to make sure I do not take the opportunity for granted. Perhaps that is why the manna only lasted for one day for the Israelites in the wilderness, so they wouldn't take it for granted. Do you remember that? If they tried to keep it overnight, it would spoil. They had to trust God would provide—day by day. They had to keep their eyes open—expectant, waiting, believing. There are a limited number of days each year when you get up and run west, and the world is fresh with dew, and pleasant and good, and then you turn around to come home, and every leafless branch and every rabbit thicket is beaded with glistening dew and the east rising sun shoots eternity through each blazing ball of light and sets your heart on fire.

In all of life, we are living within these limited windows of time, where God extends us gifts, which we receive only if we recognize them as his handiwork. Chesterton instructs us that such limits and boundaries can lead us into the practice of a pattern of praise. When we realize that everything we witness around us has been saved from the terrible wreck of non-existence, we dance with joy. "I felt economical about the stars as if they were sapphires," G. K. confesses; "I hoarded the hills." Be sober, be vigilant: pay attention.

ENTERING THE LANDSCAPE

I'd like to challenge you to begin to develop what Robert Hamma calls a "spirituality of place." Have you ever noticed how much attention Genesis chapter two devotes to describing the place where God put Adam and Eve? We are told of a garden, a garden with a river, a river with four flowing branches, each branch having a name (Gen. 2:10-13). It seems we are creatures who have been tied to land from the moment of our creation: Adam comes from the *adamah* (from the earth, in Hebrew).

So it is natural for humans to have what Chesterton calls a "love of special places." God has created us, from the beginning, with a longing in our souls for place, for hearth and home. Against the Gnostics, we affirm that everything that God made was good. Never mind Augustine's warning that any "stops" made on earth are only weigh stations on our journey to heaven. Never mind that Bunyan would have us dissatisfied with anything less than the Celestial City. The notion of the Christian as pilgrim only serves to emphasize that we do have a built-in longing to situate ourselves. The longing may not ultimately be satisfied until heaven, but even heaven will be a place. Chesterton argues "that Paradise is somewhere and not anywhere," and suggests that it will likely include a green lamppost.

A spirituality of place begins with a longing, then, to get to know a particular countryside, to enter into the painting, to sink into the landscape. God communicates to us through places, through holy places where we take our shoes off, and through resting places where we go barefoot in the creek.

As a child, when we drove long distances in our beige dodge station wagon (its back seat facing rearward), I can remember playing a game with the landscape that rushed by our car window at 55 mph. I would imagine myself in a motorcycle or car race and place myself in my pretend vehicle driving about ten yards off the shoulder of the road, in the grass or fields or whatever happened to be there. The effect was something like a cartoon scene, where I would be dodging trees, houses, and cows, and where overpasses would act as huge stunt jump-ramps to launch me sailing through the air. I mention this odd way of entertaining myself only to say that sometimes I would glimpse out the window of our racing car a place that was so beautiful I would find myself wishing I could stop and spend the day there, and just do nothing but sink into the surrounding—a slender, white waterfall, and half-way up lies a knoll of thick, green moss just begging for someone to stretch out on it; or a creek, with a huge, flat rock in the middle for a child to capture and hold all day against the Viking enemy.

Sometimes I will even look at a particularly appealing landscape painting (say from one of the Hudson River artists, or from Harlan Hubbard), and I will find myself longing to enter into the landscape—to stroll the river, scale the rocks, edge just beyond that clump of trees. I suppose some of this desire comes from the same child-like spirit within us that wants to enter and explore new worlds just by opening wardrobe doors and believing. But part of our desire to sit by a creek all day, or to stretch out on a hill and look up at the sky for hours, comes from a desire to know something so deeply that we also discover an assurance of being known.

In the summer, we used to vacation in Breckenridge, Colorado, and at the end of the road where we stayed were trails that go for miles (and I've gotten to know those trails). One summer, when it was 70 degrees where I was living in Indiana, and the cobalt blue sky was dotted with bold white clouds, I said to myself on my run: "Breckenridge isn't any better than this." Now that may sound disingenuous, but the fact is, I knew that Midwest place, and God shook it alive for me. Even after being gone for over ten years, I still know that rural road, its pastures, hills, and trees; I know the creek as a friend. There is a spot where I used to stop sometimes and sit on a culvert, and pray, and listen, and watch. I can still enter that place, that sacred space, in my inner mind and soul: I know it well, and it knows me. Why not find a place to get to know, a painting to enter—out your door, down the street, at the edge of a park in town. My hunch is that there is a longing within you—perhaps not as strong as the desire for friends, certainly not as strong as the desire for food, but all the same, a longing to experience unity with the creation, and through that unity, to taste of the goodness of the Lord.

THE PROBABLE EXISTENCE OF ELVES

Did Chesterton believe in elves? I'm serious. Because there are only a limited number of ways you can answer that question. Of course, by "elves," I am not asking whether Chesterton believed in cherubic creatures like the Keebler Elves, nor whether he believed in Rudolph's Christmas dentist friend, Hermey; nor even in Tolkien's more noble figures like Legolas. "I had seen what Virgil calls the Old Man of the Forest," Chesterton once claimed; "I had seen an elf."

Chesterton often writes about elves, fairies, dragons, elfland, bewitchment, magic and the like. But does he believe in them—that is, does he believe they are real? We might decide: No, he does not actually believe in their existence. Or, on the other side of this elfland fence, we might conclude he does believe in them, perhaps even that he's encountered them personally.

However, several options fall between these two extremes. For instance, Bruno Bettelheim, in his splendid book, *The Uses of Enchantment*, states that "when [Chesterton] says that fairy tales are 'entirely reasonable things,' [he] is speaking of them as experiences, as mirrors of inner experience, not of reality." While there is truth to this notion of a symbolic, inner psychological component to human encounters with elfland, I want to urge caution. It's easy to detour down the dismal skeptical path that considers all things supernatural (or unexplainable) as merely arising from primitive (unenlightened) mythical thinking. Chesterton, this argument would propose, preserved the kernel (the idea, moral, or spirit) of fairyland while discarding or "demythologizing" the husk (the actual story, event, or reality). The reality exists, but only as inner experience.

"The view that fairy tales could not really have happened, though crazy[,] is common," remarked Chesterton. Such rationalism seeps in as sickness. Most people who are "physically strong and [living] in the open air" do believe in fairies, he argued. "Powerful peasants and farmers six feet high all believe in fairies. Rationalism is a disease of the towns, like the housing problem." The close-minded rationalist decides, in advance, to exclude certain witnesses—as being too simple to understand what they experience. But you ought to believe the testimony of the old apple-cart woman when she mentions elves, says Chesterton, the same as when she tells you about the Duke, because "being a peasant [she] will probably have a great deal of healthy agnosticism about both." Is a scholar walled up in a room with volumes of convoluted opinions a more reliable authority? "I am forced to [believe]," declared Chesterton, "by a conspiracy of facts: the fact that men who encounter elves or angels are not the mystics and the morbid dreamers, but fishermen, farmers, and all men at once coarse and cautious...." I should add that most runners—living as they do "in the open air"—fall in this category of sane people who believe in elves. "What will the modern world do if it finds (as it very likely will) that the wildest fables have had a basis in fact; that there are creatures of the border land...oddities on the fringe of fixed laws...?"

And what if we encounter actual "evidence" of elves? Certain stretches of my run rumor such evidence—grass much greener than ordinary; trees arranged just so; cobwebs placed in inspired patterns—painted with dew and dazzled with morning sun; and a strong spirit in the air. "I was sitting the other day on a heap of stones in the Isle of Thanet," recalled Chesterton. "Not a straw had stirred; not a bird had spoken, but my blood ran cold, and I knew at once that I was in fairyland." On another occasion, when he had experienced a moon-drenched soundless world, where "frost fastened every branch and blade to its place," he wrote: "something was present there.... It was an enchanted place." Once, deep in the forest, he felt the ancient quality of faerie run through him: "an ancient elegance such as there is in trees."

If we consider Orthodoxy's clear medieval logic as helpful, then we might propose that Chesterton believes elves possibly exist; that, in fact, there's no logical necessity ruling out their existence. Recall the distinction made in "Ethics of Elfland" between necessary logic and modern science's assumption that nature always operates according to fixed "laws." If the apple (Apple) hit Bill Gates' nose, then Bill's nose hit the apple (Apple)—that is necessary logic, but fruit may float or fly from trees instead. Falling apples only implies the way things "normally" happen, "weird repetitions," Chesterton calls them. But we cannot really explain the "why"—why this "world" or "event" instead of "another," or none at all for that matter. If asked "why," Chesterton insists we must reply, "It's magic." It may be most accurate to say, then, that Chesterton believes elves probably exist—it's likely.

Chesterton did admit he was gullible when it came to elves. "The fairies like me better than [the poet] Mr. Yeats," he conceded; because "they can take me in more." Yeats "is not simple enough; he is not stupid enough." As Chesterton defenders, we applaud his childlike innocence, wonder, and optimistic faith. "I look at everything with the old elvish ignorance and expectancy." And during seasons like Christmas who can blame him. "Personally, of course, I believe in Santa Claus;" he grinned, "but it is the season of forgiveness, and I will forgive others for not doing so."

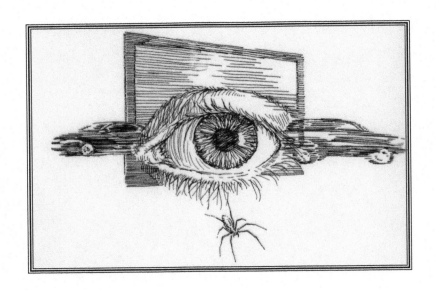

Slower Than a Speeding Car

I'd rather people call me a runner than a jogger. After all, jogging is a form of exercise for people past their prime, right? Yet, in truth, what I actually do four Midwest seasons a year when I leave my house is jog. One of the reasons why I jog instead of run is that I am learning how to slow down and pay attention to God's world. If God speaks and I am in a mad rush, how in the world am I ever going to hear?

Having grown up in one of the most beautiful places in the world—Portland, Oregon—I was not immediately impressed with the comparatively flat, and predominantly brown scenery of rural Iowa, Illinois, Indiana, and Michigan where I have lived since I was transplanted here over two decades ago. But consider, too, how most people who move to the area view this part of the country after first arriving. Normally, one sees the Midwest from a car window at 65 to 70 mph. Now, if instead of driving a car on the road, you jog right *through* the trees and fields, you gain a completely different perspective. The shades of brown here are not limiting but infinite, the textures so graceful in the wind, the varieties of grasses and wild flowers so manifold, and the landscapes so variegated in their hue and trim. Raucous, racing birds shoot through every scene. And the Midwest sky stretches out forever. In mountain country you don't see skies strewn with those lazy, dancing white pillow clouds you want to eat for dessert.

Sometimes, the run not only forces you to slow down because something catches your attention, sometimes you are squarely forced to stop dead in your tracks and hold your breath—because a bull stands in your path, staring straight at you, or you've glimpsed a fledgling owl from your periphery, or a hedge tree is shedding its leaves, or you've just lost your contact lens. I'm not quite sure how it happened. It was a fluke. I was brushing sweat off my brow, and pop, there went my contact. Screech, stop, down on all fours. Now, its amazing the different perspective you get when instead of going 70 mph, you are on your hands and knees scuffing and scrutinizing the turf. There are these tiny red spiders, and cool black-bellied ones with blue stripes, and well, you name it. I never found the contact lens, but since then, every now and then on my run, I bend down on one knee and for a moment *look through* the grass and sedges and wild flax. I know for a fact that God can go 70mph, but I'm also fairly sure he likes to speak at a slower pace.

Sometimes we erroneously equate slowing down with geriatric demise, assuming that slower breathing means death is near, or that slower driving means one's driver's license ought to be revoked. On the contrary, slowing down may actually mean more life, not less—and perhaps a deeper wisdom. Speed actually may be a formula for spiritual suicide. The pace of MTV-images, for instance, or the visual stimuli we are injected with through frenzied freeway driving, hardly encourages serious reflection of any kind; so that one wonders if faster pace actually encourages mental and spiritual lethargy. Perhaps we can begin to consider the way we look at things. Look slowly, but deeply into life. Chesterton reminds us how easily we allow our eyes to grow ever more lazy. "Let us become ocular athletes," he urges. It was Our Lord who said, "The eye is the lamp of the body. So if your eye is healthy your whole body will be full of light" (Matt. 6:22). Maybe, if our eyes were more astute, more attentive to life as gift, God would have more opportunity to transform us from within through his Light. So, let us train our eyes to see both that which is startling in the surrounding landscape and the beauty of the ordinary.

BROTHER BLADE AND SISTER SWARD

On either side of the trail as I run, tawny grasses stretch their heads above a shelf of sparkling snow. What I notice is infinite variety. Pascal suggested our world expands as much when we peer into a microscope as when we gaze through a telescope, detail dividing and expanding exponentially. Immediately, I realize I don't know the names of most of these plants. I wish I did. I'd have to research to even begin to make distinctions among them, as Annie Dillard does in her *Pilgrim at Tinker Creek* chapter titled "Intricacy."

My brain stutters. Wordless. How can I even begin to articulate the shades of brown in these winter sedges, grasses, and rushes? Color turns to metaphor: tall wide blades in hues of khaki tan, the color of desert sand or camels, fields of wheat, smooth-cut white oak, or of a lion lounging in a veldt. But the grasses join last summer's dried wild flowers, whose stems and heads stand out more darkly than the grass in tints of bronze or copper. Bordering the grassland chocolate, cordovan, and mahogany stalks emerge from tangled thickets. "To the man of our age nothing is as familiar and nothing as trite as words," bewailed Abraham Joshua Heschel. "We all live in them, think them, but failing to uphold their independent dignity, to respect their power and weight, they turn waif, elusive—a mouthful of dust." My words cannot uphold the dignity of these common stems and stalks—citizens of their own kingdom.

It's Monday, my longest run of the week, and I'm glad for that, because it takes time for something sacramental like this to sink in. There are places in his early writing where Chesterton stresses the divinity of things—the sort of awareness of the individuality of created things that St. Francis expresses through his friendship with "Brother Sun and Sister Moon." Often I find myself returning to a particular 1903 *Daily News* essay where Chesterton suggests: "there is a great pressure of spiritual reality behind things as they seem." Wait. Did a dried thistle just wave?

Lately, I've wondered about the Hasidic side of Chesterton. For the Hasid, prayer connects one relationally to all things. Think of it this way:

in Martin Buber's framework of I-Thou and I-It, no I-It need exist—all becomes a Thou, dealt with in dignity. Prayer entails relationship to all things. In *My Way to Hasidism*, Buber describes such a person of faith: The one "who in truth longs for and embraces God, sees in all the things of the world only the strength and the pride of the Creator who lives in the things." Compare that with Chesterton's essay I mentioned: "if a man, dismissing the Cosmos and all such trifles, looks steadily and with some special and passionate adoration at some one thing, that thing suddenly speaks to him. Divinity lurks not in the All, but in everything." Grasses whisper. Thistles nod. "If deep green hair grew on great hills, I know what I would do."

Of course, Chesterton always distinguished between Nature and God, never co-mingling the two. "When once a god is admitted, even a false god," he contends elsewhere, "the Cosmos begins to know its place: which is second place. When once it is the real God the Cosmos falls down before Him."

Indeed, in winter, dried wildflowers and grasses line the trail like subjects who have come to pay homage to their passing monarch. Some might see only weeds here—underbrush scrub to clear. But I begin to notice individuals among the throng: ironweed, chicory, thistle stalks and heads, milkweed pods, and bunches of blue aster still tinged with light grey—all set in a sea of sedges. "St. Francis," noted Chesterton, "was a man who did not want to see the wood for the trees. He wanted to see each tree as a separate and almost a sacred thing, being a child of God and therefore a brother or sister of man."

Brother Bluestem wore his tassels today; Sister Sedge came unadorned. They seem to have come in groups, in companies, yet sometimes evidently by themselves. The thistle delegation, standing rigid, appears to have arrived with a complaint, whereas the bluestem and tufts of beach grass both bow reverently. Some flowers don their finest hats as if celebrating a coronation; others stretch their arms out wide in petition. How far have these creatures traveled to get here; how long have they waited by the trailside for me to address them? They stand, longing to be recognized, hoping to be noticed and named. What can I offer? But what word of hope can I bring them? What *right* have I to even a parched dandelion? Unexpectedly, like Zechariah in the temple I am struck dumb. Like Isaiah, I wail, "Woe is me, I dare not speak." Wordless. Silent. Then suddenly, it clicks and I understand. All this time, I thought God commissioned me as emissary to them, like Adam assigned to name the animals. But instead, it seems God appointed them as my heralds. "There is no speech, nor are there words; their voice is not heard; *yet their voice goes out* through all the earth, and their words to the end of the world" (Psalm 19:1-2). As Chesterton recognizes, "For us the elements are like heralds who tell us with trumpets and tabard that we are drawing near to the city of a great king."

Jogging With G.K. Chesterton

More Slowly

A friend of mine described how a sports med clinic helped correct some element of his running—something to do with his stride or posture, I recall—that enabled him to increase his speed (lower his minutes per mile). As he narrated his tale with glee, one word bounced in my head like a Ping-Pong ball: "Why?" Why would anyone want to run faster, unless of course, you were competing in a race, or fleeing from rabid dogs or politicians? For most of my running "career" I've held steady at around a ten-minute mile (which I find convenient for estimating distances). I realize my pace is slower than a wildebeest in monsoon mud. I also realize running fast produces pain. In college soccer, we were expected to run two consecutive six-minute miles to make the traveling team: it hurt terribly.

At a ten-minute mile, I can pace my running—if my math is sound—at six miles per hour. That's a pretty sane speed from which to view the world and reflect on life. In fact, Wordsworth thought seven miles per hour was too fast. In an unpublished book on Lake District travel, Wordsworth pondered the tourists who asked their guide: "Is there anything worthy of notice on the road?" The Guide's first concern is to hurry his customers on their sixteen-mile excursion without stops, only letting them see what they can "through the windows of a close Chariot [a horse-drawn coach], as the several vehicles are whirled along at the rate of 7 miles an hour." And we struggle to keep our journey under 77 m.p.h.

Wordsworth likely would have enjoyed Kosuke Koyama's book of essays titled *Three Mile an Hour God*, biblical reflections on the God "who invites us in the direction of depth rather than distance" (ix). Koyama reminds us, for instance, how slowly Israel's wilderness lesson advanced—forty years slow. "The people of God were taught the truth of bread and the word of God in the wilderness as they walked three miles an hour by the three mile an hour God."

Similarly, Chesterton insisted "the real psychology of wonder depends on some return to simplicity and even to slowness." Continuously increased novelty only adds to our boredom; "and …the notion of merely going faster and faster means to this mortal life what it means in motoring—the incapacity to see anything at all, even our own speed."

A colleague of mine just broke his ankle in three places playing intramural basketball—right before he was scheduled to deliver a paper at a national conference. Watching him limp around a college campus in his "boot" illustrated how irksome it is to slow down, how awfully inconvenient. (Though perhaps, in fact, a biological survival mechanism in us fears slowing down, since the slowest person in the group is the one who will fall prey to the lions).

Yet our culture continues to equate slowing down merely with growing old, out-of-touch, and useless. Whereas, being busy, in a hurry, exhausted by our pace, serves to feed our vanity: whispering seductively that we are important, desired, in demand—even indispensible.

In reality, hurry is a form of greed, a way of chasing the tail of our mortality. "Avarice has no dreams" proclaimed Chesterton, "only insomnia." Avarice has no time to dream. I go faster because I want more; and I want more because I am afraid to slow down; because if I do slow down, I will have to face myself, my limits, my God. When we actually slow down, haunting questions of particularity surface: Is "this" enough (this day, this job, this body, this life, this person I live with)? Am I enough? Is God enough? As in the wilderness, going slow requires trust.

Thus, hurry becomes a way of denying our finitude, our creatureliness, and our continual dependence on God. "We are all beggars," asserts Johannes Metz in *Poverty of Spirit*. "We are all members of a species that is not sufficient unto itself. We are all creatures plagued by unending doubts and restless, unsatisfied hearts. Of all creatures, we are the poorest and the most incomplete."

But deep within us we do sense that slowing down can mean more, not less. Fast food often is neither fast nor food. Faster driving, on the person's bumper in front of us, does not produce any good in us. Talking faster, cramming more into a conversation with a friend, often leaves us feeling tired and not any more understood. Wayne Muller suggests that some of the best things in life can only be grown in time (slowly)—as in meals cooked with the family, making love, art, prayer and worship, long walks through the woods, or running.

Chesterton noted, "Every true English road exists in order to lead one into a dance." But we can only enter this dance with a clear head by slowing down. Then we discover we live "in relationship" to the land we traverse, as a young Gilbert once described when he was out walking: "It was a burning blue day, and the warm sunshine, settling everywhere on the high hedges and the low hills brought out into a kind of heavy bloom that *humane* quality of the landscape which, as far as I know, only exists in England; that sense as if the bushes and roads were human, and had kindness like men."

Hush

Chesterton seemed to shift into contemplative gear rather easily—sometimes by choice, but often out of absentmindedness (frequently, it seems, these cases of meandering contemplation were related to train travel, walking, or a trip by hansom cab). Consider how being forced to lie in bed led Chesterton to contemplate life's first principles and to distinguish first from second principles—second principles like when respectable people are supposed to get out of bed in the morning. In his wonderful essay, *What I Had in My Pockets* he described an occasion when he was

> locked up in a third-class carriage for a rather long journey. The time was towards evening, but it might have been anything, for everything resembling earth or sky or light or shade was painted out as if with a great wet brush by an unshifting sheet of quite colorless rain.... There was nothing but blank wood inside the carriage and blank wet without. Now I deny most energetically that anything is, or can be, uninteresting. So I stared at the joints of the walls and seats, and began thinking hard on the fascinating subject of wood. Just as I had begun to realize why, perhaps, it was that Christ was a carpenter, rather than a bricklayer, or a baker, or anything else, I suddenly stated upright, and remembered my pockets.

Reaching into his pockets, he realizes he does not know what he has in his pockets. But each item he pulls out becomes for him a symbol of something profound: of literature or commerce or art or war. In the end, the only thing he doesn't have in his pockets is the ticket for the train he is riding.

There is a way that Chesterton seems to move nimbly beyond the dullness of daily details——past the merely urgent and noisy——to the truly significant matters of life, revealing a state of self-forgetfulness that is akin to humility and very important in spiritual growth. There is something unselfish about looking out at objects and people and the world as it goes by and having an ongoing internal conversation with them. The greatest spiritual masters exhibit this trait of being able to "detach" themselves, as it were, not only from the swirl of immediate events around them, but from their own inner drama of emotions and thought, to consider matters from a broader, more eternal, more prayerful, perspective.

The same can be true for runners. While running, something can happen which is very close to contemplation, the goal of which is to detach ourselves from thoughts that crowd into our consciousness, and instead, focus quietly on the presence of God.

Running can offer the perfect setting for this kind of letting go. No phones (hopefully). No Daytimer, Palm Pilot, I-Pad. Though the sight of runners plugged into MP-3s and I-Pods distresses me, music on the run makes more sense than trying to multitask for work on the run. A friend of mine once said that his best sermons were often conceived on mile two and forgotten on mile five of his run. What a wonderful image of letting go, of trusting that if a thought is worth remembering it will return. In fact, that is the whole point of contemplation—that our thoughts and schemes and dreams are not as important as simply sitting humbly in the presence of God. "I am not proud," declares the Psalmist, "I have no haughty looks. I do not occupy myself with great matters or with things too difficult for me. But I still my soul and make it quiet."

Chesterton wrote a marvelous article during the war entitled, *The Importance of Doing Nothing*, in which he suggested it was a good mental (and spiritual) exercise to consider "the enormous number of things that do not matter." This is a good brief definition of the contemplative state, in my mind, providing that we add that the one thing (person) that does matter is God. Chesterton continues: "What it means is that it is very good moral discipline for most people to be made to realize that the world would continue to go on cheerfully if they were dead." We let go of our Messiah complex. A friend of mine told me a story about a colleague, a type A-Employee on steroids, who took a vacation and came back two weeks later radically different—not harried or anxious. He asked him what had happened. He replied, "I realized that if I died on the trip, they'd bring in some young fool who had no idea what all my files were about. He would look at them in confusion, promptly throw them all out, and start fresh. So that is exactly what I did: I threw everything out and started over."

Running can provide a kind of solitude or quiet, then, less like the monk's cell and more like the rhythms of waves washing up on the beach or the hypnotic sight of a calm camp fire. Your feet continue to keep pace with your heart and breathing in a kind of a chant cycle. What happens is that as the urgent fades into the rhythms of life, the eternal shines through the clouds more cleanly.

WHEN NATURE CALLS

Chesterton likely would have enjoyed Monty Python. One thing I'm sure of: he'd split his waistcoat laughing over Python's "Silly Olympics"—perhaps especially appropriate this year with the Summer Olympics being held in London. Gilbert's self-deprecating sense of humor surely would have identified with Python's "100-meter Race for Runners with No Sense of Direction." At the starter pistol, all the sprinters bolt off in completely different directions. That is how I sometimes imagine a jog with G. K. would turn out, glancing over my shoulder after a few minutes, expecting to see him several paces behind me puffing away, and then realizing suddenly that we took different paths from the start. Some of the "Silly Olympics" scenes are a bit dark, as in the "200-meter Freestyle for Non-Swimmers." Starting whistle; competitors dive in; camera fastens silently for a long time on the water, which becomes deathly still; until the commentator breaks in, remarking that coverage will return to the race when they begin "fishing the corpses out."

My favorite event, however, is the "Marathon for Those With Extremely Weak Bladders." As the camera follows a set of distance runners along a country road, we see one after another peel off into the bushes to relieve himself, later re-entering to catch up with the group. It's a brief, but hilarious scene.

I'm sure that serious runners, planning to finish at the front of a race, or to whittle time off their personal best, willingly suffer all sorts of torments. For us amateurs, however, a rather obvious math dictates that distance runners (it takes time to run distances), who generously hydrate if they're smart (so as not to fry their brains), cannot continue to take in fluids indefinitely without bowing, as it were, to nature's call. While certainly easier for male joggers than for females, my hunch is that I'm not the only medium-distance rural runner who finds stopping along the path necessary.

Now I admit that I've often recommended running as a potentially contemplative or prayerful form of exercise—as a doorway into a soulful silence. But what I've noticed over the years is that when "nature calls" on the trail, and I stop—then things around me also stop and I'm introduced to an even more profound silence. While it's true that running "off the grid" normally locates one in a setting with relatively less racket, nevertheless running itself as an activity carries a certain pounding rhythm and noise (the sound of footfalls, breathing, wind in one's ears, and the swishing of hi-tech gear)—a noise that is not yet stillness. And, over the years, when I've stopped—whether to drain my internal hydration system, or stretch, or gaze at a huge painted turtle sunning on the path in front of me—I've always "noticed life" at a richer level.

That deeper noticing, that more acute awareness of the simple, the beautiful, and the astonishing—lies not only at the root of Chesterton's childlike wonder, rightfully praising daisies and the greenness of grass, but also comprises the essence of prayer: "Be still and know that I am God." Can we really know anything without stopping to pay attention? Perhaps stopping like this implies a subtle shift from a self-centered perspective, allowing us to see the person or thing before us not merely as an object. When I am forced to stop I cannot help but notice and listen more carefully. When I do stop on my run, I'm aware of how infrequently during the day I allow myself to pause like this.

Maybe, in fact, we have our life's equation inverted: the very point of all our running ought to be to stop, look, and listen. Sabbath culminates creation. We don't rest in order to work; we work, run, and expend, in order to sit still and simply "be" with God.

The plot of much of Chesterton's fiction happens "on the run." Think of it: *The Ball and the Cross* becomes one long footrace, as Turnbull and MacIan attempt to outrun their pursuers: "As they were both good runners, the start they had gained was decisive." The narrative of *The Flying Inn* traces the adventures of Dalroy and Pump (pub sign in tow) winding round the rolling English road. *The Man Who Was Thursday* finally crescendos, from the criminals chasing the police, to the detectives pursuing Sunday who, "like a great ball of india-rubber," bounds away. "I have never been caught yet," declares Sunday, "and the skies will fall in the time I turn to bay. I have given them a good run for their money, and I will now."

But notice that the point of each story is not really the running, but the stopping. Turnbull and MacIan desire to stop so they can fight their duel. Dalroy and Pump periodically stop to refresh some band of locals with their store of rum and cheese. Perhaps all our running in the end only beckons us to find reason enough, truth enough, to stop for. And what do we find there in that silence? "Who and what are you?" we demand of the mysterious silence. "'I am the Sabbath,'" says Sunday, "without moving. 'I am the peace of God.'"

IT'S MAGIC!

The uproar of some Christian parents and guardians of culture over the good and evil wizardry described in the Harry Potter books makes one wonder whether the words "Christian magic" can be legitimately paired. Of course, thinkers like C.S. Lewis and G. K. Chesterton would not have had a problem with the concept of Christian magic. As Lewis insisted through the voice of professor Kirke, "Nothing is more probable." The reason Chesterton and Lewis had no qualms about the notion of magic is because they were so fundamentally committed to a supernatural worldview. If one replaces the word magic with the word supernatural or miracle, then no dilemma exists.

Conversely, the reason we are so bothered by the idea of magic is that our worldview—not the one we subscribe to in theory, but the one we practice daily—is so thoroughly naturalistic. Alan Jacobs puts it something like this: if we depict a character stepping onto a transporter beam platform, disintegrating, and then reintegrating in another spot by a stunning feat of advanced technological engineering, we stand up and cheer. Yet if one produces the same feat of disappearing and reappearing by the wave of a magic wand, some of us begin asking uneasy questions about the occult. (G. K. was familiar with the fashion of English occultism in his day and one wonders if he was at all happy at Blatchford's conversion to it). Christians claim they earnestly believe in the supernatural, but truth told, mostly live as though everyday choices produce results only in the realm of natural causes and effects. Supernatural events or phenomenon occur in a separate, nearly unconnected sphere from those in the mundane world—aberrations, which, if we recognized them, would require us to adjust our worldview (or perhaps, in the West, land us in the madhouse).

Let me cite a concrete example of running into a miracle. In the cold of winter our first year living there, we nicknamed Indiana "Windyana." One February day I was running East—directly into a gusting 20-30 mph nor'wester with a biting 38 degree rain—my least favorite running weather. I was praying for a friend named Jack, who was facing huge obstacles in his life—health problems, for one. As I was praying, and as I was fighting the icy slanting elements, I kept thinking of the passage in the Gospels where the disciples are in the boat amidst the storm with Jesus absent. There is a line in Matthew's account that reads: "and the wind was against them." So I thought of how the wind I was fighting was similar to the storm plaguing Jack. Now you can call it what you like, but as I rounded the corner of County Road 600 to go south … the wind stopped. Perhaps, surmises the skeptic, a dip in the road or a wall of distant trees briefly blocked the wind. Maybe cows nearer to the road stood on each other's backs in an attempt to reach low hanging apples and they blocked the wind. Maybe the jet stream momentarily but decisively shifted the barometric pressure due to the disproportionate number of babies born in Britain that year. In any case, I was not thinking of *how* the wind stopped; I was thinking instead of the Gospel story. Do you recall what happened? Jesus came to them, walking on the water. He got into the boat. "And he [spoke]: 'Peace, be still.' And the wind ceased." Jesus spoke and something happened.

That instant, when the Indiana wind stopped, I knew Jack was going to be okay, and I got down on my knees in the middle of a rural road and thanked God. In fact, a few weeks later, a group of friends anointed and prayed for Jack and before long, his health had taken a radical turn toward improvement.

In his masterful chapter of *Orthodoxy* entitled *Ethics of Elfland*, Chesterton argues against the materialist "man of science" who presumes that the cosmos is an impersonal machine operating according to scientific "laws of nature," or according to strict principles of closed cause and effect. The man of science assumes that this principle of causal connection is a *necessary* principle; Chesterton disagrees: "We must answer that it is magic." What causes apples to fall instead of to float? We do not really know. What causes the wind to start and stop? For all we know, the next apple freed from its limb may stay suspended in mid air like a balloon. The next gusts might start and stop in intervals exactly replicating the rhythm of Bach's *Sheep May Safely Graze*.

I wonder whether there is any correlation between the decreasing ability of our generation in the West (so influenced by Protestant collusion with the Enlightenment) to perceive the supernatural and our increasing separation of ourselves from nature and Spirit (not that those two necessarily always go together). We can fairly characterize our Western mindset as naturalistic, humanistic, individualistic, consumerist, and technocratic—in other words, as ultra-modern—having taken Enlightenment ideas to absurd, inhuman extremes. By contrast, many two-thirds world populations, more closely tied to nature than we in the urban West, have no difficulty acknowledging the miraculous in everyday life. Reports from missionaries about prophecy, healings, and prayers answered amazingly, ought to make us ask why we are so slow to perceive God's hand in our daily activity. Perhaps a good start would be to practice Chesterton's healthy phrase: "It's magic."

RUNNING INTO A MIRACLE

Was it a miracle or was it only a coincidence? A number of years ago I was faced with an important decision of whether or not to take a new job, which would require relocating in another state. As I was running and praying for some sense of confirmation, an "inner" voice surfaced with some reassuring words indicating I should take the new job.

A mile or so into the run, I happened to scan a stand of young birch trees along the road and what I saw stopped me like a brick wall. There was a cross hanging in the middle of a sea of brambles, a wooden one. It appeared so clearly to look like what a cross should look like, I immediately thought kids had constructed it for play. As I moved in for a closer examination, however, I could tell—because of where this emblem rested in the brambles—that no one could have physically reached it. Was this a message from God?

Suddenly it dawned on me: a thin sapling had snapped in several places at once, one of the pieces falling into the tangle of brush to form the horizontal bar of what resembled a perfect cross. Yet this "cross" materialized merely as a coincidence of nature, right? There was no need to consider miracles or divine influence. Instead, a natural explanation easily offered itself: the sap still ran in this thin straight limb when like a mischievous Leprechaun an unexpected freeze swelled the tree's inner fluid beyond the young bark's capacity: crack, snap, shlunk; broken branch caught sideways in a thicket. There was nothing miraculous about the incident. It was merely a matter of physics.

The modern mind fixates on the question of *how*: *how* did it happen? If we can only describe *how* the branch broke and fell into that particular shape, then our curiosity rests satisfied. We have explained. End of story. "The mechanical optimist," warns Chesterton, "endeavors to justify the universe avowedly upon the ground that it is a rational and consecutive pattern. He points out that the fine thing about the world is that it can all be explained" (*The Book of Job*).

Paulus, the eighteenth century Rationalist, engaged in intellectual gymnastics in order to translate the Gospel miracles as merely natural events. Jesus fed the five thousand when the crowd decided to share its extra provisions, moved by compassion from the example of the boy who offered his few loaves and fish. Paulus went so far as to suggest that when Jesus "appeared" to walk on water he actually walked on a kind of raft sunk a few feet under the water that the naïve disciples did not perceive. However, the explanations of the Rationalists appear more miraculous— more improbable—than if we simply took the miracles at face value. For those like Paulus who want to explain miracles as natural events, all miracles evaporate—in advance. They are ruled out from the start. No evidence could possibly be introduced to convince them otherwise. Most intelligent people recognize the unfairness of this kind of reductionism that decides the outcome of any investigation of miracles from the outset by the assumptions with which it begins. As Chesterton asserted: "If a man believes in unalterable natural law he cannot believe in any miracle in any age."

Such a dismissive reading of miracles eventually results in a position like David Hume's that insists that the parts always explain the whole. Hume would argue that once he explained sap, temperature change, diameter of sapling, and the fortunate geometric support of the brambles necessary to catch and hold the crossbar at the perfect horizontal intersection, then all is illuminated. There is no further meaning to this event—there can be no message or purpose. Chesterton would ask Hume why branches exist at all, or why the cold, or who hung the stars in place (questions God asked Job).

In Romantic response to the Rationalists, Schleiermacher claimed that all life was a miracle. Similarly every tree, each baby born, any breath a human takes is, in Chesterton's words "a great might not have been." Chesterton is almost willing to tread this romantic path—to fold all causation, all occurrences, all life into one grand miracle. As noted earlier, Chesterton exclaimed that "Divinity lurks not in the All, but in everything." Yet Chesterton understood too well the danger of sliding into an insipid pantheism that runs all existence into the indistinct splotch of a cosmic porridge. What is essential to Western orthodoxy and politics, insists Chesterton, is the notion of a transcendent deity, separate from us. "The pantheist cannot wonder, for he cannot praise God or anything as really distinct from himself."

At one level, Chesterton is simply content with mystery. The question "how" misses the point altogether. If we cannot explain *how* a miracle occurs, neither can we explain how matter holds together or why eggs hatch into birds and not into brambles. "What everybody knows is that pumpkins produce pumpkins. What nobody knows is why they should not produce elephants and giraffes." Mystery, after all, is what keeps us sane; belief in miracles begets humility and human health. At the deepest level, for G. K., the question of miracles is not about *how* but about *whom*. Both Rationalism and Pantheism remain incurably impersonal toward deity. But Chesterton affirms, instead, the Christian view that repetition in Nature has its origin, "not in a thing resembling a law, but in a thing resembling a will." Or as he maintains in *Orthodoxy*: "Magic must have a meaning and meaning must have someone to mean it." If miracles can indeed be called willful magic, magic that requires a magician, a purposive act pointing to a person, then running into my signpost cross hanging in the brambles was likely less about the new job I was considering than it was about the pledge of God's presence with me. Either way, I'd call it a miracle. "The riddles of God are more satisfying than the solutions of men."

WHEN GOD SPEAKS BACK

Does God ever speak to you directly through his creation? I don't mean *generally*—through the beauty of a sunset or through shafts of sunlight fanning out from parting midday clouds. Most of us accept the notion that the creation "proclaims God's handiwork," that through its beauty and order it conveys something to us about God's love, provision, and care for us. But I mean something more than that. What I want to ask, instead, is whether God ever speaks to you *specifically* through the creation? The Psalmist declares to God: "You make the winds your messengers, fire and flame your ministers" (Psalm 104:4). Is that mere poetic license? Potentially what is at stake is the whole issue of communication with God. If nature *is* silent, does that mean God refuses to speak? C.S. Lewis expressed to a friend "the haunting fear that there is no one listening and that what we call prayer is soliloquy: someone talking to himself." He asked, "Are we only talking to ourselves in an empty universe? The silence is often so emphatic. And we have prayed so much already" (*Letters to Malcom*). A silent universe? May it never be! If, on the other hand, it is true that God sends messages through the creation, then *how* is it true?

When I used to run each morning down my westward road in Indiana, I would see the Gatekeeper and we would talk. A tall, broad oak, dead without leaves but still standing, the Gatekeeper guards the road with one limb outstretched in salutation. When I'd pass him, he'd ask, "Who goes there?" I always responded: "Robert, servant of the king." And then he would add: "Enter his gates with thanksgiving and his courts with praise" (Psalm 100:4). You see, that's a gatekeeper's job: to ask who we are. And that's not a bad question to ask ourselves every so often. Gatekeepers also remind us that we are entering the realm of the king. And so he would remind me each day I ran to pay attention, and look, and listen, so I could be a manalive. "Oh, I get it," you say—"You're using your imagination." In George Bernard Shaw's play about her, Joan of Arc tells her accusers that she has heard voices from God. Her enemies sneer, "You know that is only your imagination." She retorts: "Yes, that is how God speaks to me." Okay, but is it really *God* speaking?

St. Francis thought so. Now we have to understand, as Chesterton reminds us, that St. Francis was not what New Age folks would call "a lover of nature," as in the sentimentalist pantheistic sense of that phrase. Instead, he thought of nature as continuously directed by God, as if by the conductor of an orchestra. "A bird went by him like an arrow; something with a story and a purpose." Perhaps birds even went by with a message. Of course, we all know Francis preached to the birds. I don't doubt, however, that he listened courteously to them as well. For Francis, insists Chesterton, these were "particular creatures assigned by their Creator to particular places" (*St. Francis of Assisi*). A friend told me that once when he was about to commit an egregious sin, he heard a thump on the house that nearly scared him to death. Going outside to investigate, he discovered a dead sparrow beneath the window. He got the message.

But *we* cannot really talk with animals can we? St. Francis assumed we could; I assume the same thing. I haven't preached yet to the birds, but I have a habit of blessing them—especially the redwing blackbirds in spring and summer. They like to let you know that you are running through their territory by scolding you. So I run backwards, and respond, and try to remember I am a guest. Occasionally, I can strike up a conversation with a red tail hawk or a chickadee.

St. Francis also knew that the created order could speak to us symbolically. As Chesterton suggested, "The Franciscan birds and beasts were really rather like heraldic birds and beasts." I was on a spiritual renewal retreat in Illinois, running one morning on snow-covered trails, and I was seeking God's forgiveness in my life. I prayed, "Lord, show me some sign of your forgiveness and love." Then I thought how silly and presumptuous that request was. God had already clearly declared that message to me through Scripture and the liturgy. Immediately, four deer bounded across the path in front of me. I stood breathlessly still. Then a red tail fox dashed through the white field on my right. "Not a bad sign, Lord," I whispered. "Thank you."

Maybe God does desire to speak to us more directly through the creation. Maybe we, with our rationalist assumptions and busy schedules, are simply not awake enough to listen, not alive enough to see. In an *Illustrated London News* essay on Herbert Spencer and sports, Chesterton asserts that Spencer's youth was misspent. "It was spent over the scientific names of things instead of over the things themselves—Herbert Spencer never saw a thing in his life; if he had seen a thing he would have fled screaming." A Christian runner might draw two conclusions from this statement: first, running through God's world might be a remedy for a generation grown dull to the voice of God; second, for those who do not have ears to hear, nor eyes to see, even a direct message from God might be rejected as coincidence, or fled from as if from a poltergeist.

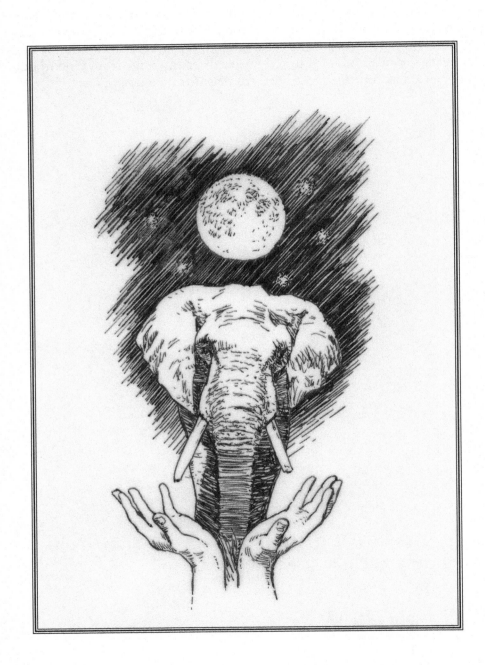

THROUGH THE DANDELIONS

One day, Anthony the desert monk was accosted by a philosopher who asked him how he managed to get along without books. "Sir philosopher," replied Anthony, "my book is the nature of created things, and it is always at hand when I wish to read the words of God." Any runner on any given day might utter the same confession. Yet nature sometimes makes for ambivalent if not confusing reading.

On the one hand, we all know the creation contains certain "lessons" which teach us about God's nature, power, provision, and design. "Ever since the creation of the world his eternal power and divine nature, invisible though they are, have been understood and seen through the things he has made" (Romans 1:20). The order and predictability of the universe seems to indicate some design behind the project. "So one elephant having a trunk was odd," declares Chesterton; "but all elephants having trunks looked like a plot." Symmetry points to purpose; progress points to personality behind the purpose.

> Nature cannot be making a careful picture made of many picked colors, unless Nature is personal. If the end of the world were mere darkness or mere light it might come as slowly and inevitably as dusk or dawn. But if the end of the world is to be a piece of elaborate and artistic chiaroscuro, then there must be design in it, either human or divine. The world, through mere time, might grow black like an old picture, or white like an old coat; but if it is turned into a particular piece of black and white art—then there is an artist. (*Orthodoxy*)

Many of us affirm that God *made* the world in a way analogous to what Chesterton is describing. In fact, theological confession of this stripe coincides with that portion of the biblical witness that declares creation to be reliable, regular, life-giving, and beneficent. A wise, care-giving Creator holds chaos, according to this perspective, at bay. People who experience life in this way are ready to affirm, "the lines have fallen for me in pleasant places" (Psalm 16:6). Incidentally, this is the world runners witness on an almost daily basis. As a result, it is relatively easy for Christian runners to declare that God cares for and sustains the cosmos. In other words, through the created order God is telling us about his goodness and greatness. The creation proclaims his handiwork.

On the other hand, the cosmos is not always kind. Consider Tennyson's "nature red in tooth and claw." In his biography of Emily Dickinson, Roger Lundin describes how nature had become mute, dark, and lifeless to many intellectuals in the post-romantic generation. Did God speak through nature? Dickinson wrote these lines:

> I could not bear the Bees should come,
> I wished they'd stayed away
> In those dim countries when they go,
> What word had they for me?
> And I, and Silence, some strange Race
> Wrecked, solitary, here.

A silent God? A silent universe? Surely not. Instead, most of us scurry to concur with the general lessons of praise and gratitude that God's world evokes. The creation is magnificent. The psalmist blurts out: "When I look at your heavens, the work of your fingers, the moon and stars that you have established; what are human beings that you are mindful of them, mortals that you care for them?" Or the Psalmist catalogues the wonders of the created order and can find no better way to end than simply crying, "Bless the Lord, O my soul. Praise the Lord!" (Psalm 104:35) It seems Chesterton had the same kind of reaction when confronted with a common weed. "Through what incarnations or prenatal purgatories I must have passed, to earn the reward of looking at a dandelion," he muses. "Man merely in the position of the babe unborn, has no right even to see a dandelion; for he could not himself have invented either the dandelion or the eyesight" (*Autobiography* 321, 325).

Some might contend that this sentiment still represents only our own wishful thinking, our solitary voice responding to what could be simply the mute and mindless forces of nature. It appears, then, that creation leaves us with a choice—will we believe or not? Pascal framed an answer to this question, claiming:

> [God], wishing to appear openly to those who seek him with all their heart and hidden from those who shun him with all their heart, ...has qualified our knowledge of him by giving signs which can be seen by those who seek him and not by those who do not" (*Pense'* 149).

In other words, if we want to believe, creation affords us enough evidence.

What Chesterton forces us to acknowledge, in the end, is that the choice before us is not between an optimistic belief in a benign creation, and a benign belief in a mechanical creation, but rather between a creation (always mysterious and sometimes terrible) authored by a benign God, and a brooding, despairing nihilism where life has no ultimate meaning. "When there is no longer even a vague idea of purposes or presences, then the many-coloured forest really is a rag-bag and all the pageant of the dust only a dustbin....[The pessimist's] philosophy of the dandelion is not that all weeds are flowers; but rather that all flowers are weeds" (*Autobiography*). Let us at least understand the choice before us.

THE LAST YEAR OF YOUR LIFE

"What would you do with your life if you knew you only had one year left to live?" That is essentially what I ask my students at the beginning of a class I teach on spiritual formation. For instance, would you still go running? I've learned that I need to emphasize that the person in question has at least "one year" left to live. When I first introduced this discussion to students a few years ago, I asked, "What would you do if you only had "a month" left to live?" A student in the front row—one who actually liked me, I think—blurted out: "Well, I sure wouldn't be sitting here listening to you." So I learned that I needed to extend the period to a year. After all, if one knows for sure that only a month remains, then the urgent tasks at hand are put aside to spend time with loved ones and perhaps set injured relationships right again. When the end of life is hypothetically extended to a year, most students still think they would drop out of school to spend time with family and friends; some put travel or other experiences of pleasure or thrill high on their bucket list; every now and then a single male student will confess he'd get married, or an especially pious one will stress the need to share Christ with others. Once in awhile a senior will declare that she would finish school if possible.

I think this exercise of telescoping time has some important ethical applications. For instance, if we knew we were going to die, we might want to put our moral house into better shape. That is what the last chapter of Lewis Smeades' book *A Pretty Good Person* conveys. Smeades narrates how his brother, Wes, was diagnosed with cancer and given about a year to live. He asked Wes what he wanted to do with the time he had left and was stunned by his brother's reply: "I want to become a better person than I've been." Smeades—a theology professor—was a bit unsettled by his brother's answer. He confesses that, at first, he wanted Wes to travel, visit Ireland, smell the flowers, see the sunsets, touch the people, live lightly—and stop worrying about things like becoming better.

Several years ago when I was pastoring a church in Indiana, a young woman named Amy set up an appointment with me for counseling. After sitting down in my office, she came right to the point: Amy wanted permission to have an affair with her doctor. This was the most interesting request I had ever received as a minister. In my mind I fumbled briefly through my Pastoral Theology class notes and textbook: "Nope, they didn't cover this one in seminary." Was she really expecting that I would write her a permission slip? Amy was convinced, of course, that she deserved it. I wasn't sure how to reply, but suddenly this is what came out of my mouth: "What would you do if you knew Christ were going to come back at the end of the week?" She growled, obviously miffed at me. Amy admitted that if she really knew Christ were returning soon, she would not go through with the affair. She ended up not doing it.

In *Man's Search for Meaning*, Victor Frankl offers a similar ethical "tool," which he calls the categorical imperative of logo-therapy. It works like this: when faced with a moral dilemma, imagine that you have already lived once, but that previously you made the wrong choice, the one you are about to make; now you are living for the second time and you have the opportunity to correct your mistake. What will you do? In Woody Allen's film, *Manhattan*, there is a great scene toward the end where Isaac, played by Allen, confronts his friend Yale for sleeping with Allen's current girlfriend: "What are future generations gonna say about us? My God! You know, someday we're gonna be like him. [pointing to a classroom skeleton] And now look. This is what happens to us. You know, it's important to have some kind of personal integrity. I'll be hanging in a classroom one day and I wanna make sure when I thin out that I'm... well thought of." This is the attitude the Greeks had toward the tragic-heroism of human life—we should make a good name for ourselves to be remembered by. That seems a bit self-serving, though. I like much better the moral of the story told about Pablo Casallas, one of the world's greatest ever cellists. At ninety-four, someone asked him why at his age he practiced four hours each day. He replied, "Because I think I can see I am making some progress." C. S. Lewis, who had a healthy theology of purgatory, expresses a wonderful thought in Mere Christianity: if I only have eighty or so years to live (and especially if I only have one year, I might add) then when dealing with a problem like my anger or my greed I can expect to make only limited progress. But if (as an eternal soul) I have a few million years to work on it, well then, I might as well get started here on earth.

What is presupposed in everything I've said so far is that we normally do not pay close attention to how we live. We constantly trade the truly important things in life—family, friends, God, prayer—for the mundanely urgent—emails, lists, deadlines, and making more money. We live our lives in a hurried blur and do not prioritize well. Or we collapse from over-busyness and "veg out" as if we'd been lobotomized. As Peter Kreeft suggests, few of us will arrive in heaven angered that we had not watched more TV re-runs while here on earth. So this "meditation" might cause us to ask what is truly valuable in our lives. Jesus, turns and asks two would-be followers, "What are you looking for?" If God, prayer, Church, family, restoring broken relationships, telling people we love them—if those kinds of things are indeed important, then why don't we begin investing more of ourselves in them? There is a story told of Augustine that describes him planting an apple orchard. A passing friend stops and asks him what he would do if he knew Jesus were going to return at the end of the day. "I would finish planting my orchard," Augustine replied. Whatever he meant by this statement, isn't it true that this is how we should be living each day—where, if we knew we would die, or if we knew the Lord would return, we would not need to alter anything. I'd still go running.

MEMENTO MORI

What I am puzzling over is how to decorate my running shoes with some form of skull. I suppose I might find something either among Halloween trinkets or in a line of children's pirate toys. My interest is not related to ancestor worship or to a remote Aztec sport where the first one across the finish line is allowed to kill his or her fellow runners and collect their bones. I am thinking rather of that fine western tradition of *momento mori* symbolized by Yorick. A grave digger unveils Yorick's skull, plunging Hamlet into brooding over human finitude. "Alexander died, Alexander was buried, Alexander returneth to dust," he groans to Horatio. Liturgically, we could say *memento mori* belongs to the season of Lent where we are reminded for the good of our souls that we are dust and to dust we shall return. In a broader context recalling one's mortality is a salubrious spiritual practice throughout the year. During the Middle Ages, a skull on one's desk served as a healthy reminder of life's brevity.

However, much of the way we regulate our day-to-day existence in American culture directly denies the fact of our looming death: our youth culture fears aging (except when it comes to good wine); the animals we eat for food are killed and "dressed" for us some place far out of sight, presented to us finally only in the most aesthetically sanitized wrappings in the grocery store; and in the end, we dispose of our aged family members in out of the way "retirement centers," dressing them up at the end with an embalmed smile as if to suggest they are merely sleeping. Chesterton insists, "We have all forgotten what we really are." All our modernist efforts to deny the true limited nature of our existence mean only "we forget that we have forgotten." "All that we call spirit and art and ecstasy only means that for one awful instant we remember that we forget." What a wonderful description of the purpose of Ash Wednesday: "for one awful instant we remember that we forget." Ash Wednesday shocks us awake to the reality of what we are and the season of Lent attempts to prolong that consciousness.

No runner can sleep the conveniently forgetful slumber of American comfort and ease. Each new run alerts the runner's mind and body to an impending death through the pain experienced. Each year we run (after a certain age) finds us a little slower, with a few more aches, carrying a few more pounds, less competitive, and happy now just to finish the run. "We are a puff of wind," sighs the Psalmist, "our days are like a passing shadow" (Psalm 144:4); a mere fleck in a drop of water may kill us, reminds Pascal. Nor is it only old age that murmurs to us of our impending demise: from birth we are a body wasting away. Jogging near a freeway one glimpses flower-strewn crosses marking those who have died in car accidents "before their time." Or you may jog through a cemetery and notice a tombstone carved with lambs, blessing infants or children who have departed this life. (This was the case for me where I lived in Reynolds, Illinois, population 600, where the cemetery—beautifully laid out on a rolling hill—served the community as walking, jogging and bike path for most of the year).

As a runner in the north winter, the icy wind slices through to the marrow, whispering coarsely in my ear, "You are like a flower of the field, blooming today and tomorrow fit for the furnace." In the deep summer days of high humidity, flies bite me awake and the turkey vultures circle menacingly as if anticipating the feast of flesh to come. Neither the black fly nor the vulture distinguishes between me and the road kill on the shoulder. Sometimes I fear it is because I run so slowly that the vultures think I am four minutes away from expiration and that if they keep a watchful eye on me, they'll gain a more sumptuous snack than usual.

During every season and in every region of the country road kill lurks on the running route as a symbol of life's limits. In Indiana opossums and frogs line rural roads; in Michigan deer, raccoon, and woodchucks; in eastern New Jersey grey squirrels. Somehow it makes sense that opossums and armadillos die on the road; they appear slower and stupider. But animals like deer or dogs (ones closer to us on the food chain) lie heaped on the road as a parable of our fragile human existence, where simply being at the wrong place at the wrong time can end everything. Occasionally one will even spot the remains of a goldfinch or hawk along the roadside unfortunately blindsided by a truck. How tragic. Today we flourish like a flower of the field, and tomorrow....

Awareness of our mortality changes the way we live and the way we think about our lives. It either steers us toward materialistic, hedonistic cynicism (like that found in Ecclesiastes); or induces in us the indifference of deep depression; or it may cause us to reexamine our lives so we readjust things where necessary, finding ourselves more aware of the daily gift of life, wonder, and joy. As Chesterton reflects:

Here dies another day
During which I have had eyes, ears, hands
And the great world round me.
And with tomorrow begins another.
Why am I allowed two?

Backwards

Cross training, as far as I can tell, is a secondary form of exercise intended to build muscles and transfer stress to a different set of joints and ligaments than those ordinarily used. So, for instance, the jogger who constantly pounds her cartilage on concrete sidewalks takes up tennis to strengthen muscles around her knees through lateral movement. Similarly, Chesterton constantly offered his readers a kind of intellectual cross training. He knew people easily slip into lazy mental habits that lead down wrong paths. People in this state need someone or something to wake them up, to stretch their intellectual muscles.

Often when I'm running I run backwards—not for a very long stretch, of course, maybe forty yards or so at a time. This habit began, I believe, as a nod in the direction of cross training, an attempt to use a different set of muscles, however briefly. As far as I can tell, it works.

In addition to running backwards, let me mention a way of thinking backwards that is productive. Chesterton, in his article *The Man Who Thinks Backwards*, argues that we must first go back if we are ever to think straightforwardly. In *Alice in Wonderland*, the queen rebukes poor Alice, crying, "It's a poor sort of logic that only works backwards." But of course logic *must* sometimes begin by working backwards in order to disclose first principles and governing premises. Sometimes even in the middle of doing something, we must think in reverse, as when C. S. Lewis suggests the analogy of a math sum gone awry: until you go back to the place where the mistake was made, no further amount of ciphering will help. Peter Kreeft explains it this way: "Philosophy, unlike science, does not go forward to discover new empirical truths, but backward to illuminate where arguments come from" (*Christianity for Modern Pagans*). Chesterton claims, "He who has thus gone back to the beginning, and seen everything as quaint and new, will always see things in their right order" (*The Man Who Thinks Backwards*). Backwards thinking thus forces us to use logic. For Chesterton, the move backwards was simultaneously a return to first principles.

We might as well admit that there is something very western and linear in this kind of backwards logic. The point of going back is to find the right way forward to the desired destination, in philosophy the "telos." "Where shall I begin?" Alice asked the Cheshire Cat. To which the wise cat replied: "Why not begin at the beginning, proceed to the end, and then stop." For the Christian, there is a telos, an end, a destination worthy of the run. For Chesterton, the only reason to go back is to find the correct path forward toward full life in Christ.

Incidentally, this logic can work with passages of Scripture or literature that are either overly familiar or difficult and remote—something I call "Backwards Exegesis"—where one reads the text line by line in reverse order. The simple process forces one to piece together the author's logic. Since you begin at "the end" of the argument, you need to examine each segment one link at a time to see where and how each one connects. Try it some time.

Chesterton knew that cultures also easily take wrong turns and need to traverse backwards to regain the correct path. Speaking of the transition in the early church from paganism to Christianity he maintained:

> It was no good telling such people to have a natural religion full of stars and flowers; there was not a flower or even a star that had not been stained. They had to go into the desert where they could find no flowers or even into the cavern where they could see no stars (*St. Francis of Assisi*).

In other words, it was no good telling the sophisticated but decadent late Roman culture that religion could be natural—natural religion had taken a wrong turn into a cul-de-sac when it should have served, instead, as a clear sign pointing to God. Religion must, therefore, return to the elemental cave and deserted desert in order to clearly regain the supernatural within nature again. We return to the deserted desert and discover that it is not at all deserted. In absence of clutter we discover presence, the Presence.

But can an entire culture ever be turned around? History would suggest not very often; nor does the daily news give us reason for hope. I just read a story in one of our papers where an "expert" boldly asserted that "premarital cohabitation has a greater likelihood to shatter marriage when partners have had multiple, serial partners." Now, what kind of logic is this? It's like saying people are more likely to die when they have had all the blood drained out of them, or they might be weaker after having lost multiple vital organs through serial diseases. Yet, in a sad way, the statement does seem to represent our culture's inability to think coherently. Obviously, we've taken a wrong turn. But we seem to lack the resolve, if not the brains, to retrace our steps, perhaps because we are too lazy. My father-in-law tells me that our culture dislikes logic for the same reason it dislikes exercise: because people mostly work out their minds today by straining their imaginations, jumping to conclusions, and beating around the bush.

If we sign up Chesterton as one of our primary intellectual trainers, we should expect to exercise some new muscles. We may end up sore every now and then, but we'll also end up where we want to go.

What if Spirituality

"If trees were tall and grasses short as in some crazy tale/ If here and there a sea were blue beyond the breaking pale/ if a fixed fire hung in the air/ to warm me one day through/ If deep green hair grew on great hills/ I know what I should do." A few months ago, I began to use two Chesterton poems for spiritual formation each day. Every morning (normally on the run) I would repeat the *Babe Unborn*—or at least those lines quoted above, plus the ending lines: "I think that if they gave me leave within the world to stand/ I would be good through all the day I spent in fairyland/ They would not hear a word from me of selfishness or scorn/ If only I could find the door/ If only I were born." Each evening, as I lay in bed, I would recite to myself lines from one of Chesterton's early notebooks: "Here dies another day/ during which I have had/ eyes, ears, hands, and the great world round me/ And with tomorrow begins another/ Why am I allowed two[?]"

Spiritual formation, as I understand it, is an attempt to intentionally form the image of God in us after the likeness of Christ; it is always a gift God gives us through His Church. We were created in the image of God, but like the Prodigal Son, we have squandered our inheritance, we have turned our back on our Father, wandering away and forgetting Him. All spiritual formation is about trying to help us remember, to come to our senses (as the Prodigal did); but sin lures us to forget. All sacramental life, prayer, Scripture, works of charity, and whispers of the Holy Spirit aim to help us remember whose children we are.

For Israel, Passover was about remembering; the golden calf about forgetting. Isn't it amazing how quickly Israel forgot? They had just been with their backs to the Red Sea and witnessed the power of Yahweh over Egypt's gods. How could they forget so quickly such an impressive display of power and providence? But humans easily forget, don't they? I'm reminded of the lines from *Orthodoxy*:

> We have all forgotten what we really are. All that we call common
> sense and rationality and practicality and positivism only means

that for certain dead levels of our life we forget that we have forgotten. All that we call spirit and art and ecstasy only means that for one awful instant we remember that we forget.

In *One Hundred Years of Solitude*, Gabriel Garcia Marquez depicts a culture losing its memory. Quickly, a plague of amnesia overcomes the entire town of Macondo. To facilitate memory, the inhabitants of the town frantically begin to label everything:

> "With an inked brush [Arcadio] marked everything with its name: *table, chair, clock, door, wall, bed*.... Little by little ... he realized that the day might come when things would be recognized by their inscriptions but that no one would remember their use... The sign that hung on the neck of the cow was an exemplary proof of the way in which the inhabitants of Macondo were prepared to fight against loss of memory: *This is the cow. She must be milked every morning so that she will produce milk*...Outside of town, stands a huge sign reading: God EXISTS. But one day, the residents will have forgotten how to read.

What an apt parable for our culture's spiritual amnesia. Most current consumerism aims to make us forget—boasting fast films, food, and cars; stimulating resorts, restaurants, and travel; and alluring attire, amusements, and personalities. Here's how it works: consumer culture constantly plays an "if only" message. *If only* I were richer, or better looking, or lived some place else, or with someone else, or had a different job, or could run faster, *then* I would be truly happy. Chesterton, in a 1934 article, identified this as a sinister syndrome in "modern civilized life," observing that "nobody is happy where he is." He suggested that much of the misery of both rich and poor comes from "that divine human illusion that *if only* they rush around the corner they will find something that is a little better" (emphasis added).

But Chesterton turns this "what if" wistfulness on its head, asking what if there was nothing? From the perspective of nonexistence, the simple grass and trees and breeze on any given spring day would appear as an extravagant luxury. Or what if I were only given one day to live? Wouldn't even the simplest moments of that day surge with meaning and immeasurable value?

Chesterton's style of spiritual formation—practiced perhaps during one's morning run—reminds us that trees *are tall* and that *there is a fixed fire in the air* to warm us; at the end of the day—perhaps when one is out for a walk—it reminds us of the miracles we saw, heard, touched, and tasted that day. Chesterton knew that this is the best way for spiritual formation to begin—with the wonder of waking up to the profound gift of life we already have, but take for granted; with the astonishment that arises when we pay attention to the world around us; with remembering what we've forgotten. Perhaps that is why Innocent Smith had to have such lively legs, why he ran and climbed everywhere—to serve as a symbol that he was spiritually awake.

THE SANCTIFIED LIST

Today's Running List (May 25, 2007): shorts—check/ Cool Max shirt—check/ shoes—check/ sunglasses, running cap, sunscreen/ triple check/ Walkman (and *Orthodoxy*, tape 4)—check/ hydrate—check/ check the Weather Channel—check/ stretch—check.

If you are an inveterate list maker like I am, it's difficult to escape this Omnipresent Creature. She especially haunts you at night just before bed, forcing a tortured decision of whether to get up and record a pressing new thought—further disturbing your fitful rest—or whether to trust God and let the matter hopefully resurface at sunrise. Sometimes she reappears immediately in the morning, sometimes she waits to surface until you are in the shower—quite often during the day she materializes while driving or waiting in line—and if you ever attempt to engage in silent prayer, she cascades upon you a ceaseless, senseless chatter. It is no surprise, then, that on the run, Madame List leaps out, darting in and out of my perspiring brain like squirrels dashing for their trees. Perhaps that is what Hamlet's ghost-of-a-father was lamenting when he cried to his son, "List, list, oh list." Maybe she stalks us even to the underworld. Where can we flee from her presence? If we make our bed in Sheol, will she find us even there?

Of course, this tells only half the story. I've been speaking, here, only of the allegedly urgent lists that resemble something like the one that chased me this morning: "Pray/ run/ doctor's appointment/ check emails/ turn in grades/ compose next semester's syllabi/ take Annesley (our daughter) to the bank/ write a JWGK article on lists/ pack for our Chicago trip/ mow the lawn/ lunch with Ken/ fish Kimberly's (my wife's) earring out of the bathroom drain/ etc." Ordering lists represents a science for people like me—a constantly evolving matter of what comes first and why, and what gets positioned last and why. You know you are in big trouble when you start creating new lists before your old lists are checked off, or when you begin making multiple copies of essentially the same list—one on a Post-It note, another in your smart phone, another on a legal pad in the car. As mentioned earlier, I've gone through all the list-keeping-devices that the market keeps producing and the commercial gurus keep recommending—from half-size legal pads, to a Daytimer, then to a Palm V, a T-Mobile MDA, and now a smart phone much smarter than me. Years ago, I even carried paper and pen on my runs so I could jot down ideas that materialized. Recall that I said I was terrified when a friend once told me that his best sermon ideas came to him on mile two of his run and evaporated forever by mile six. I carried a digital Dictaphone until I bought a phone with one. But lists are not necessarily good for me—especially if they allow me to pretend I can control the details of my life, a fact I recognize as untrue. On the other hand, God did create us in his image, granting us capacity as co-creators with Him. Does He make lists?

As Chesterton knew so well, a more positive side to lists exists. Recall the passage in *Orthodoxy* where G. K. compares the sacred "remnant" of all created things—trees, hills, stars, the Matterhorn— to items salvaged from Robinson Crusoe's shattered ship. Chesterton proposes that "the best thing in the book is simply the *list* of things saved from the wreck" (my emphasis). Calling this the "poetry of limits," he insists: "The greatest of poems is an inventory."

What one discovers on the run, then, is an inventory of things often taken for granted—the coldness of cold or the greenness of green, for instance. I was nearly completely unaware of the variety and beauty of birds in our world before I began running in rural Illinois about seventeen years ago. But as they began darting through my line of vision, I soon packed a pair of mini-binoculars on my runs, and purchased a Peterson's Field Guide, so I could spy out and identify indigo buntings, downy woodpeckers, yellow shafted flickers, cardinals, goldfinches, red tail hawks—and, more than once, newborn owls. Noticing birds soon encouraged me to better attend to the wildflowers greeting me like low lying fireworks along summer farm roads: delicate hues and petals of Blue Aster, Prairie Violet, Wild Indigo, or Pasture Rose; and flowers whose names indicate celestial brilliance, such as Morning Glory, Goldenrod, Fireweed, Sunflower, and Blazing Star. In fact, it seems that the litany of thanks flowing from any given run actually parallels biblical litanies of the creation. The list in Genesis chapter one cascades down from "In the beginning, God," and hands us ...... stars, seas, hills, and innumerable plants and creatures, all to be named, and all tumbling joyfully out of the pre-existent list in God's mind.

One of the wonderful things about God's lists in Scripture and liturgy is that their starting premise is always God's sovereign Love, His providence and provision. So next time you begin fretting and stewing about what you don't have done, or about what needs to be done, or about what could conceivably get done, point out to Madame List that God has a better list for your perusal—and that His list assures you that He is in loving control of your life.

THROUGH THE DESERT

I've always wanted to visit the desert. For some reason it holds a romance for me. Maybe my fascination with it blossomed as I heard friends recount their camping or rafting experiences in the U. S. Southwest, glowing over the still night peace, praising the splendor of cosmic horizons, describing rock shapes, flowers, and rivers not found anywhere else in the world. Isn't it remarkable that in these most insecure environments, so inhospitable to human habitation, an indescribable beauty flourishes?

I can picture myself next week on the cover of Runners World, sweaty sleek and fit for a fight, gamboling like an ancient messenger on a mission through the expanse. But for runners especially, the desert means danger. Think of movies like Lawrence of Arabia that portray some agonized soul crossing the sand, trudging desperately, with drained canteen, mirages appearing, hoping for an oasis miracle.

The closest I have come to desert running has been in the plains of central Kansas, the grasslands of Eastern Colorado, or briefly in Cairo, Egypt. In these cases I had to hydrate well and pay attention to potential warning signs (that is, I had to remind myself not to run stupid). Yet, in a way, all running is a desert experience—a fleeing from something, a running into deeper mystery, a reminder of finitude, a confrontation with our deeper self.

Jesus often went to the desert (to a lonely or deserted place) to withdraw from the crowds, to find a solitude allowing unencumbered communion with the Father. It was as if he needed to step out of the flow of events, commanding everything else around him to pause, shushing the world so he could re-focus, re-calibrate his soul, and reset his internal compass. From this perspective, the desert stands as a place of retreat and rest—a respite from clamor. We are all too busy. We constantly run— toward distraction, toward denial, away from ourselves—we are running ourselves to death. Don't we need a desert experience? Yet the prospect terrifies us.

I've always been drawn to Kathleen Norris's depiction of her move from New York City to western Dakota, as a contemplative turn. For the barrenness of the desert landscape need not indicate deprivation, but possibility as well. "A person is forced inward by the sparseness of what is outward and visible in all this land and sky. The beauty of the Plains is like that of an icon; it does not give an inch to sentimentality or romance....What seems stern and almost empty is merely open, a door into some simple and holy state." Here we encounter the desert as invitation to holy and healthy introspection.

For Israel, however, the desert also appeared as a trial—a time of sifting, of preparation, of depending on God—so that when the people of God entered the Promised Land they would remember God had been faithful when resources proved scarce. What did God provide? Daily Manna. Water from a rock. Running shoes that never wore out. Indeed, God alone was enough. Crossing the desert proved the ultimate test of monotheism: "For God alone my soul in silence waits" (Psalm 62:1).

Similarly, for early Christians the desert stretched out not simply as a place of Sabbath retreat, not just as a region of rest; rather it glared hotly as a land of deprivation where all masks melted and individuals faced God alone (in silence). The desert became a terrifying mirror. In the desert, demons appeared; nightmare ghouls and goblins (if we take seriously the apparitions of St. Anthony's temptation); sins surfaced that stripped persons naked. Like when Jacob stood by the brook, probably for the first time in his life, alone. He dreamt. He wrestled—with whom—with a man, with an angel, with his sin against Esau, with God, with himself? Yes. And ever after, Jacob hobbled wounded (not unlike a badly damaged ACL). So we use the desert (the wilderness) as an analogy for those times in our lives where we feel God's absence, or his threatening presence, less like natural storms when the bottom drops out unexpectedly, and more like being lost in confusion, like being orphaned, or like facing the abyss.

We know Chesterton experienced a wilderness abyss early in his life that caused him to question the very value of existence. Was life worth it? Much later he could paint the "cave" (wilderness) experience of St. Francis in vivid colors. "It may be suspected," surmises Chesterton, "that in that black cell or cave Francis passed the blackest hours of his life."

And though Chesterton surely felt deep pain in his later years, for instance, over his and Frances's infertility, or over Cecil's death, or over his own declining health, he never expressed such anguish in writing. Perhaps that's because he took his first wilderness experience so seriously.

Perhaps he looked deeply enough in the desert mirror to see himself for who he was as sinner, and to see who God was as God, and to recognize himself as God saw him—as God's beloved child—so that he never again need doubt the greenness of grass, or the blessedness of wind on his face, or the goodness of life.

Yea, though I jog through the Valley of the Shadow of Death … thou art with me. Let us run with perseverance the race that is set before us, looking to Jesus….

WINGS LIKE A DOVE

Sometimes, on sunny mornings when I bolt out the door for a run, my heart cries: "O that I had wings like a dove! I would fly away and be at rest; truly I would flee far away; I would lodge in the wilderness" (Psalm 55:6-7). For some people, running promises to free the human spirit, to relieve the dreary emptiness that can dampen earthly existence. Sometimes fleeing makes sense. Many fourth century Christians chose a simple but harsh life, running into the Egyptian and Syrian deserts as a way of "fleeing from the wrath to come," as a way of avoiding the corrosive worldliness of their culture. "Society," Merton suggested in *Wisdom of the Desert*, "was regarded . . . as a shipwreck from which each single individual man had to swim for his life." Henri Nouwen, perhaps, fled in like fashion—to save his own soul—when he left Yale for ministry in Central America, or when he moved from Harvard to Daybreak.

While some folks take up running as a way of managing their addictions, ironically, running can easily morph into one more obsessive idol. Jogging also can indicate a form of escapism. We run from our problems. As children we threaten to run away from home, but mostly don't; as adolescents we often play the prodigal and really do run away from home; in midlife we sometimes run from family, marriage, or other responsibilities. In his sermon, *The Wings of the Dove*, nineteenth century Anglican divine Percy Ainsworth quotes Psalm 55:6-7 cited above and cautions: "Here the idea of fleeing away [on wings like a dove] suggests itself as a possible solution of life; and whenever it comes to a man like this it is a source of weakness. It is not a desire to find the joys of heaven; it is a desire to escape the pains of earth." What is it, then, we are running from? In truth, often we are running from God.

In the same spirit of escapism, "Jonah set out to flee to Tarshish from the presence of the Lord" (Jonah 1:3). Under the glare of the divine eye he flinches: "Turn your gaze from me, that I may be glad again, before I go my way and am no more" (Psalm 39:15). In modern Christian parlance we might say Jonah sprints to avoid his cross. How often on my jogging route am I really running from responsibility? How often am I fleeing from God himself? "Where can I go then from your Spirit; where can I flee from your presence?" The answer given by the Psalmist is: "Nowhere." "If I climb up to heaven you are there; if I make the grave my bed you are there also." "If I run to the farthest end of my trail, even there your hand will embrace me." In other words, there is no place we can go where God is not already present. There's no escape. "Even there (at life's margins) your right hand shall hold me fast" (Psalm 139:10). Such an announcement can appear as comforting promise or as agonizing demand, depending on your relationship with God at the time. Discovering at the start of Psalm 139 that God searches out and knows everything about us can disquiet a person's soul.

Consider Jacob. Jacob runs graspingly his whole life—toward life and more life; that is, until his way is barred at the brook side, forcing him to wrestle with God and humans (Genesis 32:28), confronting him with both the yawning abyss of divinity and the darkness of his own soul. Jacob limps away from that race with a torn ACL; he'll never be the same. In his poem, *Carrion Comfort*, Gerard Manley Hopkins recalls a similar wrestling match with deity. After experiencing "that night, that year of now done darkness" where Hopkins "wretch lay wrestling with (my God!) my God," he moans, asking why God would hound him. Why "scan with darksome devouring eyes my bruised bones? and fan,/ O in turns of tempest, me heaped there; me frantic to avoid thee and flee?" I'd run from a God so distressingly dark myself.

Chesterton's season of running from God came in his early twenties. His *Autobiography* explains that *The Man Who Was Thursday* was an attempt to purge some of this darkness from his own soul—to "dislodge" or "throw off" this "metaphysical nightmare of negations." The novel depicts a dark God. Recall the scene at the end of the book where everyone chases after the character Sunday. Sunday looms as both compelling and terrifying, as a mystery both beautiful and dark. The Secretary finally confronts Sunday forcefully: "If you were the man in the dark room, why were you also Sunday, an offence to the sunlight? If you were from the first our father and our friend why were you also our greatest enemy? We wept, we fled in terror; the iron entered into our souls—and you are the peace of God!"

Perhaps in the end, though, what we're really running from is ourselves: the terrifying glass that reflects back to us the chasm of our own darkness, sin, finitude, and our deepest fears of rejection and abandonment. Yet our fleeing represents not only fear, but also our desire for God, who in the end (we discover through Christ and his suffering), has been longing for us even more than we have been yearning for him. We discover him running after us like the Father runs lovingly toward the Prodigal: "But while he was still far off, his father saw him and was filled with compassion; he ran and put his arms around him and kissed him." (Luke 15:20)

IN THE DARK

January 19th, a cold day for an early morning run. At 7:00 a.m. the County National Bank sign read seventeen degrees. Two pairs of socks, tights, nylon shell pants, under armor shirt, vest, heavy windbreaker, baklava, hat, ski goggles—in the dark, we resemble a special forces unit ready to break up the Columbian drug ring operating out of the village post office.

One of the benefits of living at the western end of the time zone is that by February the days already shed light earlier and last longer. It's not that running in the dark is all bad. A few weeks ago I ran eight miles solo late enough in the afternoon that my return home found me running across Lime Lake in moonlight under shining stars. That wasn't so bad. A lamp-lit evening run on a fine urban jogging path can be Chestertonian in its romance. But how awful that even on a well-lighted path in a city a woman dare not jog at dusk alone. There is something fearful about the dark, some primal threat of the unknown. What strange shapes and phantoms appear to us on an unlighted path! So the Psalmist asks: "Are your wonders known in the darkness, your saving help in the land of forgetfulness?"

When I was five I shared a room with bunk beds with my older brother Neil. One dark night before nodding off Neil taunted me saying that rats were going to nibble through our walls and then eat me. I'm sure at the time I deserved to be eaten. I cried and threatened to tell mom. As I climbed out of the bottom bed and sniffled toward the door, a crack of light streaming in from the hallway was just enough to partially illumine an old boot lying on the floor. "Look out, a rat!" Neil yelled as I stepped barefoot near the boot. Terrified, I screamed and flew back to bed, knocking my head against the top bunk and wailing even louder. I'm sure Neil deserved whatever punishment he got. What is it about the dark that worries us so? Sheol, the Old Testament equivalent of hell, is a dwelling in darkness, shadows and mud, at a deep level symbolizing death, destruction, and abandonment. Perhaps we're just as afraid of the darkness within ourselves, what Jung called our shadow self, and yet perhaps it's because in those places where we wrestle with ourselves we wrestle with God—as Jacob wrestled at the brook. Aslan is good, but of course he's not safe! In the dark we face the numinous, the holy, the boundaries of existence and our understanding.

In the mornings, running into the dark is a venture into the unknown, a leaning into mystery. Facing darkness requires trust, faith, courage. We know enough to see just what's in front of us. We venture forth and by faith venture becomes spiritual adventure. We come to a place of humility, to a knowing that is unknowing, to the via negativa where we declare our humility. There is nowhere we can flee from God's presence; he surrounds us, yet we must confess: "such knowledge is too wonderful for me; it is so high I can not attain to it." For what is darkness to God? "The darkness is not dark to you," God; "the night is as bright as the day. Darkness and light are to you both alike." So we are invited to face the darkness, to befriend it: "Deeper into darkness, closer to the light," sings Bruce Cockburn. We are invited into the "more than," into the more than we can see with our eyes, into an expanding darkness, that grows bigger and clearer only as we step into it.

Francis, at the time or somewhere about the time when he disappeared into the prison or the dark cavern, underwent a reversal of a certain psychological kind; which was really like the reversal of a complete somersault, in that by coming full circle it came back, or apparently came back, to the same normal posture. It is necessary to use the grotesque simile of an acrobatic antic, because there is hardly any other figure that will make the fact clear. But in the inward sense it was a profound spiritual revolution. The man who went into the cave was not the man who came out again; in that sense he was almost as different as if he were dead, as if he were a ghost or a blessed spirit. And the effects of this on his attitude towards the actual world were really as extravagant as any parallel can make them. He looked at the world as differently from other men as if he had come out of that dark hole walking on his hands.

How Much Land Does a Man Need?

Running on vacation—in the mountains near Breckenridge, Colorado or on the beach, Cape San Blas, Florida past eight-thousand square foot "summer cottages" (second homes for these folks)—the thought jogs your brain: how many square feet does a person need to live? Even forty thousand square foot vacation property reminds one of the question Tolstoy raised in his story, *How Much Land Does a Man Need?*—a story, incidentally, in which running figures prominently.

Pakhom lives as a successful Russian peasant farmer who owns much, yet who expresses perpetual dissatisfaction. As the story unfolds, he wants more of everything and is jealous of those around him who have what he lacks. After quickly scaling the ladder of material well being from serf to independent farmer, he hears of an area not far away with land rich and cheap. He takes a risk, sells all, and moves there. When he inquires from the local people (the Bashkirs) about the price of land, the Chief tells him there is only one price: one thousand rubles a day. Pakhom does not understand the method of calculation until his host explains the price is one thousand rubles for all the land Pakhom can traverse in a day on foot. Pakhom's eyes grow large as he imagines how much territory he can cover. Only one catch: he must return to his starting point by sundown, or he loses his thousand rubles. Early the next morning, Pakhom sets out at a brisk lick. By midday he's tired, the sun beating down upon him mercilessly, but he pushes himself harder, covering more ground. At one point late in the day, he views some low, wet ground and whispers to himself, "It would be a pity to leave that out; flax would do well there." Long into the afternoon he realizes his greed has taken him far from his starting point. He turns back and doubles his pace. He begins to trot, then to run. A tremor of fear rumbles through him as he feels his heart pounding wildly within his chest. Has his greed taken him too far?

Before finishing the story, I should point out that Chesterton never admired Tolstoy uncritically, though he certainly respected his mind. He admitted, "Tolstoy was a very great man;" "a logical man." "If Tolstoy had been my friend," announced Chesterton, "I should have boasted everywhere of the intimacy of so original and intense a mind—a man of genius who must have stimulated even when he provoked." At times, Chesterton complements Tolstoy's single-mindedness, as when he remarks, "[Tolstoy] is one of the very few men alive who have a real, solid, and serious view of life." However, Chesterton also charged Tolstoy with consistency taken to the point of oversimplification: "Everything in the world, from the Bible to a bootjack, can be, and is, reduced by Tolstoy to this great fundamental Tolstoyan principle, the simplification of life." In the end, this reductionism makes Tolstoy dangerous as a moralist, according to G.K.: "a good man who taught thoroughly bad morals."

Conversely, Chesterton recognized a legitimately "ethical and ascetical side of Tolstoy's work," which contained "a genuine and noble appeal to simplicity." What amazes Chesterton enthusiasts is the breadth of mind and soul that enables G. K. to grasp both sides of Tolstoy— disagreeing with him and appreciating him at the same time.

I am not aware that Chesterton ever reviewed this particular story, but I wonder which side of Tolstoy would have emerged for him through it—"the small and noisy moralist," trumpeting "an unmanly Puritan[ism]," or the profound writer who could intuit "the essential kinship of a human being with the landscape in which he lives."

In order to decide, we need to finish the story. Pakhom realized he had gone too far. But he was determined to get this land, so he ran faster as the sun sank low in the western sky. Exhausted, he reached the bottom of the hill, breathless, holding his thumping chest, just as the sun disappeared. He had lost. No, wait. He heard the Bashkirs cheering him on. Suddenly he realized that on top of the hill, at the finish line, the sun was still up; from his vantage at the bottom of the hill it was only the hill that blocked the sun from the sky. He bolted up the steep incline, heart and temples pounding, lungs burning. Groping and gasping, he staggered across the finish line just an instant before the sun vanished. The Bashkirs shouted wildly. Immediately Pakhom collapsed on the ground, blood streaming from his mouth. In a few minutes he was dead. His servant dug his grave, just a little more than six feet long by three feet wide by six feet deep. Tolstoy was not so pedantic as to rephrase the question at the end of the story, so I will do it for him: how much land does a man need?

In his discussion of Tolstoy, Chesterton suggested: "the bad fable has a moral, while the good fable is a moral...." I'm afraid Chesterton might count this tale as a bad fable if applied to the England of his day— as a way, perhaps, to tell a rising middle class (or a restless lower class) to satisfy themselves with less, to stop grasping for more. But if G. K. were jogging through parts of the U. S. A. today, I think he would note immediately how the shift in context turns this tale into a very good fable; indeed, a parable for the times.

AN EVER GROWING BODY OF EVIDENCE

Early on in *Orthodoxy*, Chesterton asserts the "fact" of original sin; and although certain modern thinkers deny its existence, Chesterton insists that human sin, "is the only part of Christian theology which can really be proved," something which any sane person "can see in the streets." As a jogger, one may corroborate human sin easily by noticing what people discard along the sides of our nation's roads and byways.

First, of course, we notice a special form of road rage that drivers experience when they see a person jogging toward them in THEIR lane. Whether this motorist mean streak indicates a biochemical reaction in the brain heightened in our society by violent media and computer games I will leave for researchers to decide, but the meanness seems to be increasing. For this reason, all experienced joggers run against traffic, carefully watching for the furry in the eyes of oncoming drivers, furry that just may swerve toward you at the last second like something out of a Hitchcock thriller. We joggers always reserve extra energy in our system in case we need to plunge head first into the rural fencerow or through the suburban hedge.

From the sinful driver's near Nietzschean perspective, the logic starts out something like this: this is MY lane, not yours; the lane measures just about the size of MY car, with precious little space left over for you; you are on foot, and roads do not exist for people on foot, or on bikes, or walking dogs, but for cars and trucks and buses; moreover, there is traffic coming at me in the other lane (at least potentially), so that if I have to choose whether to crash head-on into an oncoming vehicle or take you out, you'd better be paid up on your insurance premiums. In fact, if I happen to be angry today, or the least bit irritable, I may just decide to take you out anyway. Or maybe, instead of outright annihilation, I'd rather play a game of tag with you—bumping you slightly with a fender, enough to send you spinning end over end into the air like the apple core I just tossed out my window, or nicking your elbow ever so innocently with my mirror, or so crowding your comfort zone that you dive for the thorn bush on your own. Survival of the meanest was not new with Nietzsche; the Assyrians perfected the concept centuries earlier with their use of the chariot.

I might mention that runners struggle to keep one eye on the pavement beneath their feet, avoiding potholes and other hazards, while simultaneously trying to discern the mood of oncoming motorists.

Keeping an eye on the shoulder of the road exposes another form of sin with which joggers constantly deal—that of litter. Now you might well question whether or not litter could be counted a sin. Chesterton held "the worst things in man are only possible to man." True, he was referring to the human pride, perversion, and intellectual cruelties particularly evident during the waning of a civilization. Nevertheless, litter is something only possible to man, because of course, animals do not really litter or foul their nests like modern humans—maybe only because they cannot create synthetic, non-biodegradable materials. Thus, litter indicates both the rational side of humans, able to transcend environment, and yet the bestial side so addicted to appetites and passions. What a difficult time we have preserving the balance of our souls within our environment.

At the very least, we could contend that roadside litter illustrates Chesterton's thesis of original sin as a demonstrable doctrine—in that litter discloses a culture's clandestine sins. Each day I jog, I come across the secret or not so secret addictions that people have thrown out of their 55 m.p.h. car windows.

Most litter neatly falls into the first three categories of the seven deadly sins—gluttony, lust, and greed. Beer and liquor bottles of every socio-economic stripe line our nation's rural gravel roads and city suburban paths; glitteringly bright Bud cans glint menacingly from the most remote lake bottoms and creeks in our parks and forests—revealing our frenetic attempts to divert ourselves from deeper soul questions. We anesthetize our hearts with drink and drugs. Recall Chesterton's suggestion that we thank God for beer and burgundy by not drinking too much of them. Few modern Americans preach self-restraint as successfully as G.K.

If we could argue that abuse of liquor counts as a form of gluttony, then we also ought to consider the fast food sacks blobbed along the road edge, waiting for cars to explode them, thus sending cups, straws, wrappers, lids, and the last few uneaten french-fries peppered through the landscape. Our litter, like landmines, assaults every humane sentiment—a witness to our food addiction, an addiction making us as wide as whales and as sickly as beached whales.

Our culture's preoccupation with sexual titillation appears to runners sometimes in the form of discarded condoms or (oddly enough) underwear, but most often in the form of pornography that someone has become bored or angry with and thrown out his (not her) window, having missed the ditch it was intended for, leaving it in the low grass for the inevitable adventurous child to ferret out.

When we stop to notice, the sin of greed stares back at us from earth's ravines: from those spots where we dumped what we coveted so dearly yesterday, but threw out today after purchasing the latest, newest, nearly improved version. In the Midwest, plastic Wal-Mart bags hang high from hundred-year-old oak trees like the pocks from some fatal plague. The "creation groans" for redemption, for the day it will be liberated from our dumped stoves, refrigerators, and tires, from the glare of glittery aluminum cans and the plastic containers that will never disintegrate this side of the New Jerusalem. Our souls, too, groan for liberation from bondage.

Once again, Chesterton hit his mark when he swore that human sin, "is the only part of Christian theology which can really be proved," and the jogger, the hiker, even the casual walker, collects day-by-day an ever growing body of evidence.

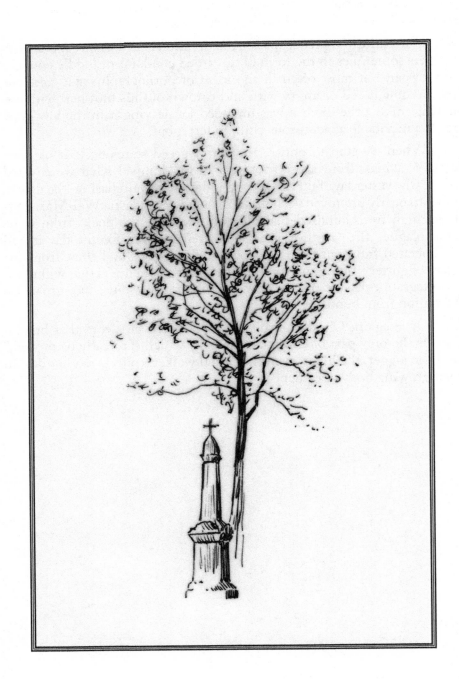

PSALM 1

On my run, trees frequently capture my imagination—ancient gnarly oaks that look as though they have migrated recently from Fangorn, tall stately fir that look as if they might guard an Elfland castle, or (much rarer) groves of white pine that seem to invite runners in for shade and who knows what mischief. Also I think often of Psalm 1 and of trees planted by streams of water, "which yield their fruit in its season. In all they do, they prosper, and their leaves do not wither." I want to become like those trees, not like the fall corn stubble that the wind drives away.

Notice also how this first Psalm, the prologue to all Hebrew and Christian piety and prayer, begins with a prohibition: "Happy are those who do not...." Human happiness, or better, blessedness, depends on the ability to "not." Eugene Peterson suggests the obvious but profound truth that humans are the only creatures with the ability to say no. Chesterton insists that certain prohibitions are woven into the very fabric of the world.

> For the pleasure of pedantry I will call it the Doctrine of Conditional Joy.... The note of fairy utterance always is, "You may live in a palace of gold and sapphire, *if* you do not say the word 'cow'"; or "You may live happily with the King's daughter, *if* you do not show her an onion." The vision always hangs upon a veto. All the dizzy and colossal things conceded depend upon one small thing withheld. All the wild and whirling things that are let loose depend upon one thing that is forbidden.

One can almost hear the echo of Moses' great final speech to Israel, "Choose life, so that you may live long in the land!" Everything that makes for human happiness, then, depends upon our ability to comprehend the veto, the prohibition, and respond appropriately.

I wonder as I run past spruce, poplars, and Bob Coppernoll's apple orchard whether I can somehow better learn to practice this skill of saying no? As a species we do not have a very good track record if one examines history. Recall that the very fall of our race into sin occurred through just such a failure to say no (notice too that a tree was involved!).

In Genesis 3, Eve knows the prohibition well enough; she repeats it to the serpent (Gen. 3:3). But she allows herself to be convinced otherwise: "God knows that when you eat of it," cooed the serpent, "your eyes will be opened, and you will be like God, knowing good and evil." No more prohibitions; no more question marks; no more unknowns; no more nos. By eating the fruit, Eve was rejecting God as the one who decides what is good and evil, putting herself in God's role instead.

The problem is this, if we follow the serpent's line of reasoning, a kind of reasoning that too often runs its circuit through our brains, we suddenly work our way down a path of exceptions to the rule. Perhaps that's what the author of Psalm 1 also had in mind. The Psalmist warns against the slippery moral slope that begins with someone merely taking advice from the wicked (the level of listening to and entertaining wicked thoughts); but which then proceeds quickly onto the path that sinners tread (now actually putting the thoughts into action); and which finally ends up with the person sitting in the seat of scoffers (settling into a sedentary lifestyle of habitual sinning). It should be pointed out that neither level one nor level two (taking advice or treading the sinner's path) appear satisfying at the time one is pursuing them; one is irresistibly drawn toward level three, toward total immersion in sin and self.

Saying "No," in contrast, is an affirmation of boundaries. And as Chesterton recommends, boundaries bring health, happiness, wholeness, and sanity. If we are to find happiness, we must adhere to certain moral limits. But the limits, the prohibitions, should not burden us with what we cannot have, but instead fill us with joy for what we do have: "Keeping to one woman is a small price for so much as seeing one woman," Chesterton exclaims. "To complain that I could only be married once was like complaining that I had only been born once." Chesterton's Doctrine of Conditional Joy states plainly: "You may live happily with the King's daughter, *if* you do not show her an onion." We tend to notice only the prohibition, only the one thing withheld, even as Eve obsessed only on the tree of knowledge, ignoring the rest of that great garden. But notice the promise beyond the prohibition: happiness with the King's daughter! Most modern consumerism complains about what is desired but not yet owned. Much of Chesterton's writing could be portrayed instead as a litany of praise for what we already have.

By saying "No" at the right time, in the right way, for the right reason we actually unleash a power that participates in the undoing of Eve and Adam's sin. In Eve's garden there were two trees planted by four rivers: one was the tree of knowledge, the other the tree of life. Much later in time, another tree, the one that stood starkly on Golgotha, began as a tree of death. On that tree Christ, God's Son, died. But, as many medieval mystics depicted it, the Rood became the *arbor vitae*, the tree of life, the budding cross, signifying to all the particularly joyous work this second Adam had accomplished and offering a new Spirit empowering us to say no when appropriate.

The Distributist Jogger

I just returned from five weeks of summer traveling. Customarily, I took time to jog in each location of my family's two-legged tour, first through Seattle, Portland, the Olympic National Forest, and then into Eastern Kansas and South Eastern Missouri. The scenic highlight of them all was running on the beach of the Olympic Peninsula (parts of Seattle and Portland ranked a close second). In fact, since wherever I travel I also run, I've been able to run in some remarkable settings: beside the Rhine River in Switzerland, up historic Breckenridge mining trails in the Colorado Rockies, through Alaskan fireweed, across beaches in northern Chile, and along the trails that run beside St. Thomas University where the American Chesterton Society once held its annual meeting. Yet no matter how picturesque or beautiful, no terrain in the world offers as fine a jogging route as my current run around Lime Lake just outside Spring Arbor, Michigan. And I'm willing to defend that assertion fiercely.

It's true, that in every place I've lived in the Midwest over the past sixteen years, the jogging routes have improved with each move (so don't mistakenly think I'm another deluded optimist). The Illinois landscape where I began my jogging addiction was astounding for the first mile that ran through Melvin Curtis's fields, but the rest of the run consisted of fairly dull squares of treeless farm road piled with too much loose gravel for much ankle support. My Indiana routes improved with more trees and hills and, at the turn-around-point of one route, a muddy slow winding river. In Michigan, however, I not only enjoy more rolling hills, and a lake, but enormous hundred year oaks along one mile that form a canopy of shade in the summer.

As I said, I'm willing to wager that my route in Michigan is superior to any other route in the world. I'm boasting the attitude of what I would call the Distributist Jogger. Part of what Chesterton aimed for with his position of Distributism was not only "one man one house" in the strict sense of each citizen owning private property, but even more the goal of bestowing human dignity and thus full civic participation. When I own my own piece of land, I experience a sense of belonging and I am willing to invest loyally in the local political community and even fight to defend my soil if necessary. This is what I mean when I tell my friends I am a Distributist Jogger. I'm fiercely loyal to my running route—no less than Pericles was loyal to Athens. But loyalty need not imply narrowness. As James Schall stressed in a *Gilbert* magazine article: "unless we see and love our own nation, we cannot see why other people might love their own nations" (*The Last Refuge of the Globalist*). Though I am loyal to my running route, I'm still willing to join you on yours.

My mother is a good example of this kind of militant loyalty to a location. We lived in Portland, Oregon beginning when I was five, and my mother also had grown up there. When I went to college in Seattle, mom constantly compared the two towns, touting Portland as the more civilized and refined of the two and describing Seattle as the brasher and more industrial. After college I moved to the East Coast but received weekly propaganda in the form of articles about Oregon and phone conversations embedded with arguments delineating the superiority of life in the great Northwest. Admittedly, here was an element of a mother's instinct to have her brood near, but also the human instinct to defend one's turf. "It is the idea," Chesterton reminds us, "pursued by all poets and pagans making myths that a particular place must be the shrine of a god or the abode of the blessed" (*The Everlasting Man*). (Portlanders declare that God rested there on the seventh day because He found it so pleasant). I have no doubt that my mother would be personally willing to fight Canadian tanks or Californian helicopters if her hometown were invaded; I think she also would debate the governor of any other state on the superiority of Oregon on all fronts.

I'm the same way when it comes to my jogging route: I could go on all day piling up reasons why it is incomparable to all competitors. First, Michigan offers four distinct seasons. Why would anyone want to skip a single one? That would be like a hobbit skipping a meal— hobbits were made for eating, and we humans were made for the seasons. (Incidentally, anyone who wants to run where it is always only warm simply lacks courage furthermore missing the opportunity to wear the wonderful winter gear of silk long johns, running pants, wool socks, layers of material that wicks away sweat, wind shells, gloves, baklavas, and ski goggles, while also missing the chance to witness the glories of drifted snow, silver thaws, and water in frozen rills tumbling sculptured in magnificent layers.) Second, where we live in Michigan, water springs abundantly and the treescape gleams with green all year round, presenting a bucolic, rural beauty varied by lakes, thick wooded trails, a wetland bird sanctuary, tree-canopied dirt farm roads stretching through rolling hills and fields, yet not steep enough to cause runners gratuitous pain. Deer, hawks, cardinals, and wild turkeys reside all year round; bluebirds, and thirty other species of songbird, a variety of migrating fowl, and sandhill cranes arrive for nesting in spring and stay through fall. Third, people are attached to this northern soil, adding to its particularity and personality. As Chesterton describes, landscape "moulds the men…, it clothes and informs everything" (*Importance of the Knowledge of Landscape*). The people here grow in and with the soil. Jogging by the hundred-plus dairy cows at the William's family farm always brings a smile, but waving to John and Brent Williams as they pass me on the road in their tractor or pickup—and having them wave back—is an even happier occurrence. Beaming Bob Copernoll, who makes his living in the country dealing in antiques and collectibles appears as no less a part of the scenery than the two classic barns down the road or the white swans that appear for spring and summer.

When, in his discussion of Distributism, Chesterton spoke of the "homelessness of Jones," he was insisting that every Englishman deserved a home. But he could not have imagined Jones having once won for himself a home, growing indifferent to it out of inattentiveness, becoming a stranger to his own hearth. This is the larger Distributist message of Chesterton's novel *Manalive*. Innocent Smith, the main character of the story has a home, but he has to "break out" from his home in order to find it; he has to leave and return again in search of what he has lost, hoping to see it this time with fresh eyes. He fears he will fall into an unknowing trance. He hopes to awaken to the richness of his own backyard. "If we were really besieged in this garden," he tells a friend, "we'd find a hundred English birds and English berries that we never knew were here."

This is precisely why the jogger becomes territorial—because the land he traverses does in some sense become his land. He may not own it, any more than a New Yorker can own Times Square or Central Park, but in terms of actually experiencing the turf and being attached to it— knowing its birds and berries—he knows it better than anyone, except perhaps the farmer who tills its hills and hunts its hollows. Particularity of place is what the jogger recognizes. Regarding landscapes, Chesterton averred, "there is, *in the place itself*, something more, which makes all the difference." There is a mystical element in all landscape, "that 'something more' we all feel when we travel, if we travel at all intelligently" (*Importance of the Knowledge of Landscape*). The jogger, runner, and hiker all know this "something more" within the landscape. Chesterton insisted that you couldn't know the Alps from maps and books: "You must traverse them." (*The Landscapes of England*) Maybe the reason some people are not willing to defend their country these days (even intellectually) is because either they realize they own no part of it (they have no "stake"), or because they have grown so detached from it that it hardly seems worth the trouble.

A LANDSCAPE WORTH DEFENDING

Do we have a defensible landscape in our country? What I mean to ask is whether we embrace the idea that our landscape is at all costs (or in any way) worth defending? I'm not speaking here about nuclear silos or anti-aircraft guns. I like to consider myself a Distributist Jogger. A Distributist Jogger is someone who, although he likely does not own his own jogging route, is willing to defend the land and landscape precisely because he knows it so well that he's become attached to it. G.K. commented once about a gardener he hired: "He possessed the garden intellectually and spiritually, while I only possessed it politically." To run the land is to possess the land spiritually. Distributism insists that attachment to land breeds a sense of belonging and allegiance, which, in turn, creates a willingness for individuals to engage in the local political process and perhaps even struggle to defend the soil. A true appreciation of land may motivate us "to devote [our] remaining strength to bringing about a keener sense of local patriotism," as King Auberon whimsically proposes in *The Napoleon of Notting Hill*. So, as a Distributist Jogger, I'm fiercely loyal to my Michigan running route—just as Pericles was loyal to Athens in the face of what was perceived as Spartan aggression. "Because of the greatness of our city," Pericles proclaimed, "the fruits of the whole earth flow in upon us;" moreover, there is "beauty in our public buildings to cheer the heart and delight the eye day by day." (Thucydides, *The Peloponnesian War*). I might even suggest that runners along different Michigan running routes take up banners, coats of arms, and gathering cries.

Now apart from the possible though unlikely need to guard our local soil by taking up arms we may frequently be called upon to defend our ground intellectually. As well as fortifying Athens with walls and navy, Pericles, in his famous *Funeral Oration*, was arguing on behalf of a culture—a way of thinking and living in the world. But do we have any geographical culture in America to defend? Could one be motivated to defend a strip mall? What ideas of value undergird our current mass culture's use of public space? Will Italian Americans rise up to fight for their local Olive Garden, or Texans rally to liberate a besieged

Texaco station? Would Pericles send up a cheer for the arrival of a new Greek fast food chain in town? Imagine the Spartan-Athenian alliance system breaking up—after their military successes together against the Persians—because the Athenians were planting Wal-Marts in their colonies threatening the viability of the local Spartan Dollar Stores.

Vast tracts of suburban and semi-urban wasteland stretch onward in this country where no running routes worth defending exist. Why is that? In his book, *The Geography of Nowhere: The Rise and Decline of America's Man-Made Landscapes*, James Howard Kunstler depicts what much of America's living and working space looks like:

> The jive-plastic commuter tract home wastelands, the Potemkin village shopping plazas with their vast parking lagoons, the Lego-block hotel complexes, the "gourmet mansardic" junk-food joints, the Orwellian office "parks" featuring buildings shrouded in the same reflective glass as the sunglasses worn by chain gang guards, the particle-board garden apartments rising up in every meadow and cornfield, the freeway loops at every big and little city with their clusters of discount merchandise marts....

Kunstler describes ours as "a landscape of scary places, the geography of nowhere, that has simply ceased to be a credible human habitat." Chesterton perhaps anticipated the rise of such industrialized wastelands when he exclaimed, "travel, in the true sense, has become impossible in the large urban or urbanized districts. There are twenty ways of going everywhere, and there is nowhere to go" (*The Meaning of Travel*). In contemporary urban settings like ours it is nearly impossible to run, let alone live—unless maybe you need to run for your life. In contrast, Chesterton recalled an English era "in which most people knew well some one landscape of their own." In the England of Chesterton's day, rural folk knew their land because they saw it unfold before them as they traveled slowly along the roads. But "a man in a town sees nothing at all," laments Chesterton. "He has no horizons—especially a man in one of the great modern towns, a journey out of which is an affair of hours" (*The Landscapes of England*).

I hate to admit it, but in our tiny town of Spring Arbor we have a Golden Starches. Yet I cannot imagine the surrounding farmers rising up to defend either it or the new strip mall recently built (though, unfortunately the town's children might). Recall that Chesterton once described a journey where he thought he was sailing to New England only to discover he had landed in Old England. Imagine instead my embarrassment if I set out to defend "my town's" McDonald's with pike and pitchfork only to discover it was the McDonald's in the rival town down the road. I was merely confused, not from too many miles run that week, but because all fast food places are indistinguishable. Would, instead, that we could proudly exclaim with Pericles, our town's culture "is not copied from those of our neighbors: we are an example to them rather than they to us."

The Similitude of a Dream

One day last week something very odd happened while jogging. A car passed by—that was not unusual; that happens often on the run—but instead of speeding off round the bend, it slowed, as though the passengers were scanning for a deer in the adjacent field, and then it stopped altogether. Doors opened and a family emerged, surprise on their faces, the dad carrying the youngest on his back, mom holding the hands of the two older children, both still under ten it seemed. As they approached me on the shoulder, I expected them to disappear down a hiking trail, or into a thicket to pick blackberries or wildflowers, but they just kept coming. "Out of gas," remarked the father as he passed, and I thought he smiled a veiled but knowing grin. Then, whether I dreamt, or whether the nitrogen had been spread too thick on the fields that year so as to muddle my thinking, other cars passed, sputtered, and slowly rolled to a halt. And I realized something strange was unfolding—not merely the result of gas prices through the ceiling again. This time our oil-dependent economy had gone belly up; the wells had run dry; the automobile was going the way of the dinosaur. People—young and old, families and singles, in pairs and groups, of all different shapes, sizes, and colors—were all stepping out of their cars—walking; some loping or running toward me. My first thought was to protect myself, to hide somewhere safe, for surely this meant violence. The comfortable American cannot lose his or her means of transportation and be expected to accept this fate nonchalantly. For most Americans, a car symbolizes livelihood, independence, even identity. So peering out from behind a tree, sweating and panting as quietly as I could, I noticed groups of people gathering—either stationary in a knot of compressed human figures, or walking together in groups. Yet they were talking; not arguing and threatening as I had expected, but chatting, remarking on the number of goldfinches they'd seen, or the effect of unions on the local school district, or whether or not to plant a garden this year, and if so, what to plant. In a sudden flash of insight I understood: people had slowed down enough to begin thinking like human beings again. Then, as if time were a street that I was lifted above so I could perceive what was occurring further down the line, I saw people stepping out of their cars. Vehicles were pushed or pulled by teams of people to mammoth lots where they were abandoned.

Perhaps what astounded me most was how people interacted, nodding in earnest, asking about one another's children, painting houses for the elderly. And they walked; and they watched. For the first time in their lives townspeople noticed that there were elms on Elm Street and that the Bank building on Main displayed neoclassical columns gaudily disproportionate for a bland one-story building. For the first time since anyone could remember parents walked their children to school. But since schools for most families had been too far away to reach on foot, many parents began to teach their children at home what their parents had taught them when they were still too young to go to school: how to read and write, how to listen and think, and how to respect elders and show courtesy. Since most people were not willing to walk more than a mile or two at once (and since the price of a good horse or mule was now twice that of a Mercedes) all manner of local business began to flourish: bakers, butchers, hardware, and grocery. People collaborated over their chief concerns: food, fresh water, shelter, possible defense. A militia was raised replete with banners and hauberks. Local elections were held. Foreign coffee disappeared. Starbucks boarded up its windows. So neighbors schemed together on how to produce homegrown teas. Television vanished overnight and in a fortnight professional sports and the pornography industry collapsed; town gossip, now in high demand, arose as the addiction of choice.

But though this looked like Utopia, I knew the bloodbath was coming—plague, foreign invaders, famine or natural catastrophe and the momentary cooperation would quickly turn into an apocalyptic power struggle over resources. For a moment the slowing down, the localization of commerce and politics, the increased personal interaction, made so much sense, and then I began to awaken, drenched with sweat, my head splitting and spinning, lying face down in the dirt with the sound of a motor running much too close to my ear. I'm in the operating room, I thought, and they are going to surgically remove this dream from me. "I'm sorry," chirped a sinister voice. "I said, I'm sorry," he repeated. "Say, are you all right? I didn't see you on the shoulder as I came around that curve. I think I ran you off the road. I don't think I hit you directly— but your head is bleeding a little. Can you stand?" I stood and steadied myself. "Yes," I quavered, I'm okay, I think. I think I'll be alright." "Good," came the confident reply. Either he was an agent of the devil or my imagination tricked me, but I swear as he hopped in his car and sped off down the road he turned and beamed a ominous smirk my way.

CIVILIZED JOGGING

When I ponder civilized jogging, my mind immediately leaps to some of the routes I have run from the Annual Chesterton Conference at St. Thomas University. You can run about two miles up Summit Street, with its wide plush median, towering shady evergreens, and sumptuous brick Tudor homes, shining with leaded glass windows and slate roofs. Or if you descend the hill behind Brady Educational Center to Mississippi Boulevard, you can connect with a first-class bike and jogging path glistening with civilization at every turn, incorporating a street bike lane for the stream of wiry cyclists speeding past in their slick, colorful gear. The well-constructed sidewalk lanes post signs for safety and etiquette, like State Statute 169.222: "Combined Path: Bicyclists Yield To Pedestrians"; another adds: "Give Audible Warning When Passing." How civilized! How genteel! Both Summit and Mississippi also sport a symbol of civilization close to Chesterton's heart: lampposts. Especially at night, lampposts facilitate civilized jogging.

But we must guard against facile consumerist definitions of civilization—as if the close proximity of Starbucks indicates "higher culture." Or as if civilized jogging were equated only with paths like the one running north-south along Chicago's Gold Coast overlooking Lake Michigan.

Yet one sometimes might legitimately link certain *so-called* human advances with what we think of as civilization. Since ancient Sumerians invented writing, the wheel, and the lunar calendar around 3500 B.C., the notion of civilization has implied the development of certain "technologies"—irrigation or aqueducts (if not strap-on hydration packs), literature or means of communication (if not **Runner's World** magazine). So Chesterton admits that civilization sometimes may be deduced by its absence, as when the Romans withdrew from Briton: "What the decline did involve everywhere was decivilization; the loss of letters, of laws, of roads and means of communication, the exaggeration of local color into caprice" (*A Short History of England* 434).

Thus, one may define civilization partially by equating it with human achievement. In this sense, civilization originates as a gift from God. One could refer to Genesis chapter one to uphold this confident vision of humans made in the *Imago Dei* as co-creators, or to Genesis two where our species received instructions to tend the garden and subdue creation, to train vines and harness streams. Some folks might even point to Plato's Athens, David's Jerusalem, Peter's Rome, or Calvin's Geneva as evidence of the human potential to create a city set on a hill. The difficulty, however, comes when optimists argue that civilization ineluctably advances. But does it? In fact, "the progressives believe [the cosmos] is a clock that they themselves are winding up," chides Chesterton. Shall we indeed boast that we can "build ourselves a city, and a tower with its top in the heavens" (Gen. 11:4)? Pierre Durand in *The Ball and the Cross* echoes this faith: "[he] believed in civilization, in the storied tower we have erected to affront nature, that is, [he] believed in Man" (95). Following this logic, jogging would be a grand sign of the advance of civilization. Only the most cultured peoples of the globe, only the richest, smartest, and most successful, could allow so many of their citizens to burn calories in such a frivolous way.

"Pessimists," in contrast, "believe that the cosmos is a clock running down," observes Chesterton. One does not have to rummage through the book of Revelation to champion such an apocalyptic outlook. In Genesis four, Cain kills his brother Abel; then he goes and builds a city (Gen 4:17). In fact, violence lives at the heart of society. Historians tell us that grain surplus induced the initial rise of civilizations. With a surplus of stored food, nomads settled down, allowing time for invention and trade; but when they did settle down, they had to protect their surplus from marauders—military and government were thus conceived. Think of the notorious cities throughout history that have become emblems of cultured opulence and civilized cruelty: Sodom, Nineveh, Babylon, Nazi Berlin, modern Amsterdam, and New York City. With the crimes of the Renaissance in mind, Chesterton averred, "Men like Savonarola are the witnesses to the tremendous psychological fact at the back of all our brains, but for which no name has ever been found, that ease is the worst enemy of happiness, and civilization potentially the end of man." From this angle, jogging might stand as a sign of civilized decadence and demise. Imagine the foreboding as the Four Joggers of the Apocalypse run pallidly past your house: war, famine, pestilence, and death.

But Chesterton rejected both optimistic and pessimistic explanations of civilization. Instead, he maintained: "Civilization is not a development.

It is a decision. It is the decisive people who have become civilized." G. K. chiefly hopes to avoid the simplistic scheme that touts civilization as a mechanical process for which humans are not responsible. "All this talk about optimism and pessimism is itself a dismal fall from the old talk about right and wrong. Our fathers said that a nation had sinned and suffered like a man. We say it has decayed, like a cheese." In contrast, Chesterton supposed "[our] own decision might have something to do with [our] own destiny." Running could serve as a symbol, in this case—almost as an allegory—where Jane Jogger wakes from her cultural illusions of security and laces up her shoes as if she were finally willing to put forth some effort for social, political, and moral reform.

EMPHATICALLY

"I told my wife you look like Tom Cruise," I blurted to a passing runner. He seemed nonplused. I had felt an urge to make some human contact since I'd seen him so often on the jogging path but had never spoken. Next time we met, he reigned in his dog and remarked, "My wife laughed when I told her what you said." Now I was nonplussed. A few weeks later I realized I had confused facts and faces: I had said "Tom Cruise," while the gentleman looked remarkably like a paunchy, unkempt version of Tom Hanks. No wonder his wife was amused.

How do we communicate when encountering a colleague in the hallway or standing behind a stranger in the grocery line? It's a significant question since our fast-paced culture increasingly reduces our communication with others to blips of texting and twitters, sound bites and mumbled grunts. Chesterton always affirmed that words matter. "Why do we choose one word more than another," he asked, "if there isn't any difference between them? If you called a woman a chimpanzee instead of an angel, wouldn't there be a quarrel about a word? If you are not going to argue about words, what are you going to argue about? Are you going to convey your meaning to me by moving your ears?" In linguistic theory our "throw away" comments about sports or weather belong in a category called "phatic communion." Phatic communion represents a form of pre-symbolic language replacing earlier communication accomplished through gestures, words or phrases used to fill awkward silences. This meaningless banter emerges when people interact in such close proximity that gestures (a wave, nod, or wiggle of the ear) won't suffice and where the relationship "glue" is not strong enough to bear the weight of either symbolic language or silence. To use symbolic language in such a case might obligate us to go beyond the surface, which could prove uncomfortable. The arbitrary phrase has no real meaning, but is employed instead to ease an awkward silence. "How about Manchester United beating Chelsea last week?" "Corn looks good this year, doesn't it?" "Hear a storm is supposed to blow in." Sometimes Phatic language takes on a terse or even pessimistic tone as

JOGGING WITH G.K. CHESTERTON

in the caricatured Minnesotan vernacular. Erik: "How ya doin', Sven?" Sven: "Could be worse."

For years my wife, Kimberly, and I have noticed phatic language among joggers. Take Ed, for instance, who farms nearby. We would see him walking toward us in the morning two or three times a week. Though not much of a talker, Ed's winking sense of humor gradually became apparent. He'd say things like: "Better pick up the pace if you want to make it home by lunch," or "You two are slowing down in your old age." If he saw me running alone, he'd snicker: "What! Did she finally leave you?" or "Looks like she outran you today." More recently we have encountered a gentleman riding a recumbent bike. Whenever we pass him, he sings out his mantra: "Beautiful day, beautiful day" (always repeated twice—as though part of the liturgy). Of course some of the best phatic language comes "pre-packaged." My favorite line comes from my father-in-law. As you approach him, he grins: "You always see your best game when you leave your gun at home."

Seven years ago, when we first began greeting Ed on the road, I discovered a dueling side to phatic communion on the run. The brief amount of time to respond and impromptu nature of the engagement presents a challenge of wits. Unless you initiate you have no idea what is coming which forces you to respond on the spot. We were walking the loop of our subdivision last night (about "dark-thirty" as my father-in-law also likes to say) and we saw some neighbors approaching, a couple in their late sixties. I shot first: "Do your parents know you are out this late?" On the next lap she quipped, "What's wrong, can't find your house?" The aim is to be creative while avoiding a critical or disparaging spirit. This morning an elderly man on a bike, whom Kimberly and I have not seen for some months, commented to us both: "You sure are running her hard; look how small she's getting." On the return leg of the run we passed again, but I didn't notice him until at the last second I yelled, "You must be running for Congress!" As he cheerfully nodded agreement, Kimberly chimed in: "Well, I'm voting for you."

Phatic communion on the run helps me recognize the power of even the smallest word-encounters. Each passing phrase illustrates, first, how dear meaning is to our species. "It is impossible for anything," insisted Chesterton, "to signify nothing." Even more significant, however, is that each human being we meet offers an opportunity for blessing another. As Our Lord teaches us, there are no throw away words, no throw away people.

FOOTBALL

Even before English and French, football embodies the clearest international language—which of course singles out North Americans as cultural isolationists. I'm not speaking about American football, as in "da' Bears," but about soccer (henceforth translated as football), the only real world sport. You might legitimately ask—why bring up football in a column about Chesterton and running? Great question!

Let me cite three reasons. First, football belongs to G. K. because G. K. was a Brit and for Brits football stands alongside religion and politics (the two topics Chesterton cared most about) as one of three things worth fighting over. Second, football belongs in this column because as far as running goes, more running normally takes place for a footballer than on all but the most vigorous jogs, seven miles is the average for a player during a ninety minute match, and at a pace and intensity of sprint that would be fatal for the average jogger. Third, I was actually jogging when I saw them playing football—really! My route in Prague that week had been to dodge through the morning pedestrian traffic and ascend the park called Petrin Hill. At the base of this small mountain, I had already noticed what looked like a fenced-in small soccer court with goals and a surface I could not distinguish. It had been empty all week but today some older men (my age) "knocking the ball about." Being an aggressive American abroad (translate that how you wish), I asked as nicely as I could in sign language if I could play.

At that point these ten Czechs had a perfect five-on-five organized and could have taken my request as a manifest insult, a diplomatic blunder, or a faux pas worth ignoring altogether. Citing UEFA football etiquette or NATO fine print, they might have drawn and quartered me on the spot or boiled me in Czech dumpling soup. But instead, with a chivalry as complete as if hosting the Holy Roman Emperor himself, they adopted me onto one team, letting a player from that team sit out as a sub.

They were brilliant players and though I could not even understand their names in Czech, we all understood each other perfectly well—all eleven of us—when it came to space, moves, patience, and passes. A beautiful dance it was, too, as we sprinted, laughed, yelled, and slid on a surface resembling a clay tennis court.

When I had to excuse myself before the game ended, I tried my best to thank them for their courteous welcome of a stranger from the USA. But my gestures could not convey the deep sympathy and appreciation I felt for them. They, too, were glad I had played. They were even accepting enough of me to invite me to their pub at noon—a date, unfortunately, I could not keep.

Had this been the only time I'd been received by fellow footballers abroad, I might imagine it was only a happy yet haphazard occasion. But actually, this represented the third such event. The first occurred in 1993 in Pachica, in the Atacama desert of northern Chile, one of the driest regions in the world, some spots never having recorded any rainfall. I recall the eerie midnight bus ride through winding mountain roads, a full moon illuminating from the shadows what looked like a lunar landscape. Three days later when our "mission team" played football against the locals—a mix of Chilean construction workers and Mapuche Indians indigenous to the Andes—the sand surface looked and felt no less lunar than the night we arrived. But again, the football was the same. Never mind the size of the goals, or the fact that my Spanish then was worse than my Czech today, or that we played directly next to a graveyard absolutely surrealistic with its combination of wood pole crosses and garish plastic colored wreaths. The universal language of football remained the same: the opponents "bravo" at a move well made or at a goal well earned; the recognition, as with musicians or dancers of score or choreography that speaks universally.

The third occasion was best of all—an experience so heavenly I will sketch it briefly using symbols and metaphors (the language we reserve for our most cherished ideas). It was the first week after our arrival in Switzerland. We would be staying for a year. In a scene similar to the one with which I began this section I saw a dance, asked those with shining robes if I could enter in, and they not only said yes, but gave me a robe too, adopting me for the year, and presenting to me, at the kickoff of the final game of the season, a bouquet of flowers and captain's armband. (They even assigned me the penalty kick awarded our team in the game.) If the field at that point was not paved in gold, I could not tell the difference.

What if the whole world played (or at least watched) football?

Let's see, who would be missing from that equation? What if football language made sense around the globe? Perhaps with God's grace we could move back to a time of international empathy and understanding; not so Utopian as before the tower of Babel, of course, but prior enough to global imperialism where duels could be fought between the parties really concerned and jousts and wars could be localized again. Perhaps if we also encouraged co-ed football we might witness a revival of that other noble institution of combat and negotiation that Chesterton upheld so staunchly: marriage.

The Omen of the Dog

Running paths can provide an endless stream of interesting people to contemplate—especially on crowded weekends. The path I normally run, located two miles south of town, stretches 10.5 miles through a fairly dense area of wooded Michigan farmland. Such a rural setting is not as well traversed as a typical urban route, but on Saturday afternoons or on a warm morning I pass numerous people walking their dogs. On these occasions, deciphering pet and owner together serves as a wonderful diversion from aching ankles and high-strung hamstrings. We like to accept the truism that dogs resemble their masters, but like our children, pets often reveal more about their owners than we like to admit.

Chesterton, of course, loved dogs. "I happen to be awfully fond of dogs," he remarked. In his essay *On Keeping a Dog*, he mentions "the innovation which I have of late introduced into my domestic life ....in the shape of an Aberdeen terrier" (named Quoodle). Like owner, the dog in his story basks comfortably in front of an evening fire.

As the last of six children, removed in age from my next oldest sibling by some years, I grew up with a golden retriever as constant companion. We were both introverts. The picture in Chesterton's Father Brown story, *The Oracle of the Dog*, therefore, of "throwing sticks into the sea for [the retriever] to swim after" reminds me of the same game I played at the Oregon Coast with my dog Duchess as we jogged the shoreline. Occasionally, on my local run, I will see dogs swimming after sticks in Lime Lake.

Chesterton speaks correctly when he claims, "a man ought to have a dog." (I'd add, "...and a dog to run with.") There is something right about the relationship between humans and dogs. Chesterton indicates, for instance, that dogs understand that we are human: "my dog knows that I am a man ....it is written in his soul." In other words, the dog does not mistake master for some evolved monkey or bundle of electro-jived protoplasm. Thus, humans love dogs because dogs somehow comprehend us. "They're marvelous creatures," suggests Fiennes, in *The Oracle of the Dog*; "sometimes I think they know a lot more than we do." Surely that is true regarding the olfactory factor. As Quoodle sings: "They haven't got no noses/ The fallen sons of Eve .../ And goodness only knowses/ ....The Noselessness of Man." If dogs exhibit intelligence, however, I am equally prepared to admit that my dog remains to me largely a mystery.

We thought about buying a golden retriever again six years ago and then decided on a Bijon Frise (a more Quoodlish breed: good for the house, not so good for running). While Father Brown declares that "a dog is an omen," we have discovered that our dog, Tess, has become a sort of mirror for us—not always a pleasant realization.

Of course, our pets reflect us. As I run past dogs with their owners, certain similar features leap out for comparison. We have all seen a petite person cradling a Poodle, or a dour person pulled by a Doberman, or wispy figure with a Whippet, but I'm talking about what our pets announce about our deeper habits and commitments. For example, I recently met a woman with a hugely obese black lab, the dog so overweight he could barely walk. Now, the lab did not create this situation. I'm sure the hound was not sneaking off for doggie-treat fast food before bedtime. Perhaps the abuse of the dog has roots in the woman's inability to love her self. Or what about the enormous energetic brown lab in our neighborhood, wedged tight in a tiny house all day with little or no outlet, and who, from the sound of his bark, seethes with anger? Perhaps his owner feels similarly trapped, stifled, turned in upon himself in his frustrated corner of life.

Or what about our dog, Tess? Tess of the Moore-Jumonvilles. Tess thinks the world is a lollipop, licking everything and everyone. Perhaps she stands as an embarrassing sign of her owners' neediness, calling out, "Please, love me." What is worse, however, is her chocolate addiction. In the past three years this nine-pound ball of non-shedding fluff has repeatedly broken into backpacks and purses to devour someone's daily supply of chocolate. Tess started out on a low dose of M&Ms, but as our family chocoholic compulsion escalated so did her level of tolerance. She now relies on dark chocolate as her drug of choice—when she can get it. Friends assured us that dark chocolate would kill her, but she has built up immunity. We try our best to keep bags on tables and doors closed when we leave for the day, but Tess sniffs out squares of chocolate from two floors away, hauls my backpack off a chair or table, unzips it like Flambeau, and noses out and consumes the handful of Dove Darks I have stashed—sometimes while we're in the adjacent room oblivious to the crime. Tess does not have a conscience to help her do otherwise. She will never give up chocolate for Lent or decide to replace her chocolate addiction with yoga or running. She remains a creature of habit while we possess the freedom to choose. Yet she's such a natural burglar it makes me wonder if I can train her to develop a taste for diamonds.

VOTING BOTHERS

Starting in our subdivision on the west end of our town of five thousand, I normally jog three-quarters of a mile before I reach Teft Road and the start of what I'd consider a country road. It's in town, naturally, where I pass rows of strategically placed election signs, jostling one another as if there were a real choice before the American voter. Sometimes I dream of re-writing Robert Frost's poem so that the ending reads "I took the road less traveled/ and it made no difference whatever." I'm not advocating a cynical indifference that whines, "Why bother to vote?" But along with Chesterton, I want to protest vehemently against the "low choice" (if not "no choice") voting offered the American public. "The trouble is simply that they are not two parties, but one party," contends G. K. Perhaps we should call it the Two-in-One Party. Why, for instance, don't Third Party candidates today get a spot on televised debates? Why do we still retain an antiquated winner-take-all Electoral College so easily abused by political power groups instead of shifting to a one person, one vote system? Why do we continue to allow finances to clog campaigns, a state of affairs which converts candidates into fund raisers and which lobbyists so eagerly exploit? Isn't the present system merely geared to protect politicians and the wealthy class? The two choices voters face today merely offer variations on the same theme.

> We have not got real Democracy when the decision depends upon the people. We shall have real Democracy when the problem depends upon the people. [The problem] is not the quantity of voters [suffrage], but the quality of the thing they are voting about. A certain alternative is put before them by the powerful houses and the highest political class. Two roads are opened to them; but they must go down one or the other."

I'm reminded of a question game I used to play with my daughter Annesley that turned absurdist like this at times, offering a adamant non-choice: "Would you rather eat a hot fudge sundae or a bucket of hot coals?" The choice is so obvious that it presents no viable option. Another variation suggests a double non-choice: "Would you rather do your jogging underwater this morning or on your hands?" So this year, the candidates will once again sing silly songs to us that purr: "Would you like your personal liberties violated for impure motives or would you like them protected by the government?" Most of us would like liberties protected, thank you very much. "You find out the necessity of liberty as you find out the necessity of air," advised Chesterton—"by not having enough of it and gasping."

Another form of this false-choice equation poses two unthinkable options: "Would you rather unilaterally attack other nations for dubious reasons or would you like your home town annihilated by terrorists?" If it is just the same to you, Mr. Party Pants, we'd like to explore other alternatives, thank you very much. After describing a false choice presented by British statesmen of his day between "Socialism and some horrible thing that they call Individualism," Chesterton remonstrated: "I'm not saying that any of these are right, though I cannot imagine any of them could be worse than the present madhouse, with its top-heavy rich and its tortured poor."

Perhaps the most common option politicians tender the public today presents a carefully crafted choice where both alternatives benefit the Two-in-One Party. "For the powerful class will choose two courses of action, both of them safe for itself," bewails Chesterton. It's as if I were to give you a choice between two pre-selected jogging paths, between the Green Path and the Orange Path, but where my friends and I owned both paths (and the drink concessions along the paths). "I have given you a choice, a chance to vote," insists Mr. Party Pants. Yet both paths are strewn with the identical hotel chains and fast food franchises; this does not look like much of a choice to me. "But those on the Green Path sell green Gatorade," persists our Political Patriarchs, "and those on the Orange Path sell orange Gatorade." Yet the same group of privileged proprietors own both the Green and the Orange establishments are owned by. If I stop for any refreshment on either path, I'm feathering the same political nest. "The highly astounding result is this," argues G.K:

> that the government (and especially representative government)
> now actually exists to protect those very abuses which government
> (and especially representative government) was actually created
> to prevent. The plain, natural history of all political institutions is
> that you want a policeman to keep his eye on the traffic, but also
> want somebody to keep his eye on the policeman.

What we need are more numerous options today, not fewer. "And as for the fanatical conflict in party politics," cries Chesterton, "I wish there were more of it." Unfortunately, our populace is being lobotomized slowly by a consumerism bent on entertaining itself to death. In fact, politicians encourage us to ignore any real complexity in political and economic issues. What would it take for a change in our political rut? It would require first that we woke up to the problem as described by Chesterton. Second, it would require a counter-cultural effort—a grass roots organization that fostered personal self-sacrifice and true leadership; which possesed a blue print from a Master Mind. I know of only one institution in our world that could offer such resources.

Through History

I sit in a park on Petrin Hill in Prague enjoying more leisurely the path and landscape I jogged yesterday, sometimes walking straight up the steep incline, sometimes sitting as I write. Much that I see, I find familiar: the dandelions, daisies, and Queen Anne's lace look like what you would see in Indiana or Illinois; the slope of the hill and mix of evergreens and deciduous might be located in Portland, Oregon; the breeze in the leaves blows the same as elsewhere. The squirrel I must admit looks more European—a little frowsy-haired and more chestnut colored (is he Irish, I wonder) as if to match the orange tiled roofs that dominate one's view of old town from here. The flies assault less violently than Michigan—maybe they are non-union flies, or perhaps they're only taking the traditional European long lunch. Of course, all these landscape features signify mere incidentals. But are the people here any different—the Czech people, say, when compared with Michiganders or Seattleites or Chicagoans? Of course differences exist: historical differences, differences of culture, language, and custom. The squirrels or buttercups may also display differences; differences to analyze, categorize, and record. However, I've been told that the squirrels on Petrin Hill have yet to record their history; whereas, the real differences between human families, tribes, and nations always begin with history.

Chesterton frequently builds his cultural analysis upon historical insight. He knew that all good historical thinking required a careful balance between critical (not necessarily skeptical) inquiry and empathy. Critical inquiry (a gift from the Renaissance) gives us a way to distinguish between our age and any other. For example, in the Middle Ages, painters, failing to comprehend the unique traits of past eras, portrayed Caesar Augustus in medieval armor, and perched the Christ child on Mary's lap seated on a throne in a gothic castle. The medieval painter did not agonize over accurate history. By contrast, Renaissance artists hurried to return to Caesar his traditional Roman toga and to place Christ again amidst animals in a straw strewn stable.

Beside me now, running as far as I can see, stands a twenty-five foot fourteenth century stone wall, notched along the top with a rampart for soldiers to fight from. Surely I would not find something like this in Michigan (though we have some noteworthy forts made of wood). History in Prague runs much deeper than occupation by this or that regime: it runs deeper than Nazi or Communist atrocities, deeper than the Hapsburgs, deeper even than the early Christian missionaries Methodius and Cyril who first brought the creed and alphabet. There is history, too, that I run through on my rural Michigan route—past the site, for instance, of a Potowatami village that New Englanders and New Yorkers coming west first encountered when they began settling the region in the mid 1830s. Of course, history spreads much thinner in Michigan. I recognize the historical differences between Prague and Pontiac as clearly as I recognize the huge gap that exists between the Czech language and my brain. "To compare the present and the past," suggested Chesterton "is like comparing a drop of water and the sea."

Chesterton knew how to make historical distinctions clear. In **Saint Francis of Assisi**, for example, he takes enormous pains to convince his readers that something new and wonderful was occurring in the thirteenth century. Chesterton writes as a master of sound historical generalization. The sky must be painted with broad strokes, he maintains, before estimating the lone figure beneath that sky.

G.K. understood, however, that critical analysis which recognizes the historical distance between distinct cultures and periods can easily erode into an acerbic skepticism. As a child, Chesterton was told that the notion of General Wolfe quoting Gray before his assault on Quebec was a myth, but as an adult learned it was true. Skepticism had been needlessly skeptical. Historical realism, for Chesterton, did not mean the same thing as naturalistic "scientific empiricism." Realism meant putting things in perspective. "Realism is the art of connecting everything that is in its nature disconnected. But to do this properly a man must be a great artist rather than a great liar." Chesterton noted that a school of history existed "which might be called anti-romantic; and it is perpetually occupied in trying to explain away the many romances that have really happened."

But G.K. also knew there must be commonalities between past and present and between adjacent cultures or no understanding at all would be possible for us. Perhaps this came from his Thomistic realism which insisted that truths were truths no matter what age they occurred in—a truth at high noon remains a truth after your evening meal, whether you call that meal dinner or supper, whether you eat pizza or potato dumplings. Things really do exist. Marble chariots atop buildings or flanking maneuvers by armies are no less real if called by different names.

Running, then, might be contemplated historically in that nearly everywhere one runs—whether Prague, Peoria, or Peking—one is running through history. Yet normally in our culture we don't percieve this. For us, whether we stay home or travel, our minds normally don't grasp how different we are from past cultures, or how much the same.

JOGGING WITH G.K. CHESTERTON

Under Suspicion

I cannot speak yet about other European nations, but having been in Prague a week now I have a theory that Czech people are opposed to anyone running as an amateur, at least on Czech territory. Of course, Czechs, emerging as a race of noble athletes, welcome serious running—as in the Prague marathon, or as in Martina Navratilova's accomplishments on the tennis court. If you are familiar with the traditional Czech diet (packed with enough cholesterol and carbs to make even the most slothful consider exercise as a remedy), this unofficial cultural stance against jogging might come as a surprise.

Yesterday, on my morning run crossing the Legii Bridge on my way to climb Petrin Hill, a young, tall, smartly dressed Czech businessperson gave me a look that registered in my blinking brain as odd. I could not quite translate what his eyes flashed, but I've noticed since that joggers appear as an enigma to Czechs. (I might simply deduce that I am witnessing an urban phenomenon—something one might expect to find in the heart of New York City or Paris—namely, that urbanites deem it odd for anyone to dodge through crowded streets packed with pedestrians—for what purpose? After all, city dwellers get their exercise by walking almost everywhere. In my own defense, I would explain that I was only jogging through crowded streets *en route* to Petrin Hill Park in the same way a New Yorker might jog up Broadway to reach Central Park.)

Now Czech, a notoriously difficult Slavic language, has seven cases replete with corresponding masculine, feminine and neuter endings (whereas Latin boasts six, Greek five, and German only four). My head spins just overhearing what I cannot understand. Therefore, when it comes to declining Czech facial expressions I claim no certainty. Yet, I think I can parse a few of the countenances I have encountered while running in Prague. First, one discerns a visage of apprehension.

Czechs are justifiably wary of runners because of their national history. Since at least 1939, the majority of those "on the run" in Prague have been "labeled" as very bad people, either fleeing Nazi or Communist "authorities," or running from legitimate police as pickpockets. Another group, however, everyone readily recognizes as good, Innocents such as children or supposed Idiots, who run because, as Chesterton insisted, they cannot help it—because at the foundation of the universe God placed a fire of newness within all things young that mirrored his image. At least one more category of runner would be completely acceptable to Czechs—those sprinting, parting crowds, leaping curbs, making moves David Beckham himself would admire—to catch a tram. Czechs might appreciate my running if they were convinced the end result was reaching work on time. But as I flash along the cobblestones of Prague (just under the speed of sound) in slick black shorts and crisp New Balance shoes, I am obviously neither child nor tram chaser. But since the Czech Republic truly enjoys a fair-minded, highly educated populace, I might receive a better hearing from them regarding the heresy of running than some of my fellow Chestertonians would grant me.

I would not, however, want to discourage the Czechs from suspicion. As a culture, they deserve a measure of guarded skepticism: they ought to remain as wary of the West today as they still are of the East. Like the Sirens, Western capitalism lures from every shop window in Prague. To really understand my meaning—to understand anything about the Czechs—one needs to appreciate their history, which from its roots intertwines with the history of Europe at every turn. The Czech people have maintained a spirit of intellectual and moral independence in spite of domination by Magyars, Austria-Hungarians, Nazis, and Communists. When they re-invented democracy at this crossroads of West and what was recently the Soviet Block, it was a playwright-poet they elected as their first president—Vaclav Havel (a decision Plato would applaud). But as I write this, Havel is out of office and suffering ill health. Who will provide the international political savvy necessary to juggle the pressures and interests of Germans and North Americans, NATO and EU? Who has the stature to shape a moral grounding capable of withstanding the McDonaldization of the Czech soul?

Chesterton himself never made it to Prague—though he was invited, and though many of his books were translated into Czech. "You will find here so many people who cherish you," pleaded Karel Capek, the Czech author. But by that time in their lives (1927) Gilbert and Frances were avoiding most trips, trying to settle into a quieter domestic life in Beaconsfield. Had he visited Prague, Chesterton would undoubtedly have been welcomed as a hero like he was in Poland. Would that the Czechs could rediscover him today! He might just provide them the precise balance they need between tradition and legitimate skepticism, between appreciation for the ways of the old world and a brand of democracy that truly sets free.

Hope for the Coming Collapse

Unless you observed carefully you would not know that the trail I run was once a railroad line. The woods and fields look as though they've always stood there; no tracks stripe the path. But perhaps if you scanned through the oaks, maples, and spruce alongside the path, you would spy small telegraph poles leaning at intervals like ancient wooden crosses. Passing them, I sometimes feel as though I am running through the ruins of some collapsed civilization. "Can you tell me," the president of Nicaragua asks the urbane Barker bluntly, "in a world that is flagrant with the failures of civilization, what there is particularly immortal about yours?" It's a question we ought to ask ourselves.

Recently, my friend Dean gave me a book I did not have time to read—James Howard Kunstler's *The Long Emergency*. I like Kunstler's writing, and I like Dean, so when I opened it up and found the following Chesterton quote penned inside the cover, I felt I should at least leaf through it: "It isn't that they can't see the solution; it's that they can't see the problem." I was hooked after page two where I read: "If I hope for anything in this book, it is that the American public will wake up from its sleepwalk and act to defend the project of civilization." *The Man Who Was Thursday* reminds us that most reflective cultures fret over the possible demise of society: "One of the most celebrated detectives in Europe has long been of opinion that a purely intellectual conspiracy would soon threaten the very existence of civilization." Though Kunstler disavows any conspiracy theory, his thesis is no less bleak. He argues that the end of the world's cheap oil age is upon us, signaling the disintegration of American consumptive suburban life as we know it. Europe, with its mass transit and more concentrated populations will fare much better. In a recent magazine interview, Joseph Pearce made a similar point: "As I've said on numerous occasions, the present system is ultimately unsustainable."

Reading Kunstler's book reminded me of a paper I had written in seminary twenty years ago on the same topic (before the discovery of North Sea oil). Here is one of the conclusions I drew:

Shortsightedness and greed, fed by increasing competition, has combined to bring about a very explosive situation. This profit mentality is summarized well by the words of the 1969 Saudi Petroleum Minister, Yamani: 'We want the present set-up to continue as long as possible ....' In other words, those who control the resources are going to 'ride the horse till it drops.'

I was surprised to discover Kunstler agreeing with me: "[Those in control] will not surrender to circumstance until it is simply no longer possible to carry on [until after the horse collapses], meaning there is not likely to be any planning or preparation for change." Perhaps we are avoiding facing the coming collapse because we are so afraid. More likely, we are blinded by our greed. "History teaches that men and nations behave wisely," counseled Abba Eban, "once they have exhausted all other alternatives."

Yet, surprisingly, Kunstler is not completely pessimistic about the future of civilization. In fact, it pleased me that both the critique of American culture and the prescription for a cure offered by *The Long Emergency* parallel Chesterton's wisdom in *The Outline of Sanity*. Against the bluff of the big shops and the mania of unrestrained consumer capitalism, Kunstler suggests that American suburbia needs to be retrofitted "into the kind of mixed-use, smaller-scaled, more fine-grained walkable environments we will need to carry on daily life in the coming age of greatly reduced motoring." Those places to which we can jog, in other words, may soon define the parameters of our community.

Kunstler's insistence on impending cultural collapse would not have surprised Chesterton in the least. Once, when he was stuck in a cab in a London traffic jam, he began musing on the fall of civilization. "Communications may break down, and men be forced to live where they are as best they can." That sounds like a line straight from *The Long Emergency*. G.K. continues, "I think how probable, after all, is the prospect of a relapse into barbarism." Sounds depressing, doesn't it? Not in Chesterton's mind. Collapse offers some hope—for "by this broken road simplicity may return."

> Man has before now broken down in the elaborate labors of empire and bureaucracy and big business and been content to fall to a simpler life. He has been content to picnic like a tramp in the ruin of his own palaces....We will not be downhearted. Our cities may also be deserted and our palaces in ruins; and there may be a chance yet for humanity to become more human.

What a beautiful idea—that in slowing down we may become more human; that in being forced to work together locally we may become more relational; that in growing our own food, and teaching our own children we may discover a joy that easily surpasses the lures of consumerist consumption. Small may become beautiful after all. As author James Baldwin remarked, "I'm optimistic about the future, but not about the future of this civilization. I'm optimistic about the civilization which will replace this one."

SAVING CIVILIZATION

Jogging today in south-central Michigan, one notices signs of a crumbling economy—houses for sale as people flee in search of jobs, boarded up warehouses and churches, and crumbling roads as the tax base shrivels. As Detroit's auto industry falters once again, all Michigan shudders economically. Sometimes it feels like jogging through a tottering civilization.

Chesterton understands history, so he knows that even spiffy civilizations come and go. "The story of the earth is a stratification of such inventive civilizations that stopped dead or were broken off short." And yet he remains an optimist. "I have two reasons for doubting this doom," he boasts: "first, because Christendom has gone through such dark ages before, and always shown a power of recovery; and second, because I do not believe in doom at all." At least part of Chesterton's optimism lies in his conviction that the Church can play a meaningful role in conserving and restoring civilization. One might reasonably wonder, however—when our economy finally does implode—what today's Church will have to offer.

Long before Edward Gibbons **Decline and Fall of the Roman Empire**, intellectuals argued that Christianity caused the fall of Rome or that it contributed to its demise. William Manchester, in *A World Lit Only By Fire*, serves as a recent proponent of this view:

> I share [the] conviction that 'a realization of the power and import of the Christian Faith is needed for an understanding of the thoughts and feelings moving the men and women of the Middle Ages'…, but I do not see how that can be achieved without a careful study of the brutality, ignorance, and delusions in the Middle Ages, not just among the laity, but also at the highest Christian altars. Christianity survived despite medieval Christians not because of them.

Historian Justo Gonzalez proposes the opposite thesis:

> It would be a long time before Western Europe could once again

experience the political unity and relative peace that it had known under Roman rule. It would also take centuries to rebuild much that had been destroyed, not only in terms of roads, buildings, aqueducts, but also in terms of literature, art, and knowledge of the physical world. In all these fields it was the church that provided continuity with the past: she became the guardian or civilization and of order. In many ways, she filled the power vacuum left by the demise of the Empire.

Chesterton offers essentially the same point in **Orthodoxy**:

[In] history I found that Christianity, so far from belonging to the Dark Ages, was the one path across the Dark Ages that was not dark. It was the shinning bridge connecting two shining civilizations. If anyone says that the faith arose in ignorance and savagery the answer is simple: it didn't. It arose in the Mediterranean civilization in the full summer of the Roman Empire.

Chesterton grew tired, it seems, of rationalist critics who charged Christianity with producing only weakness, superstition, and cruelty. Once, in a debate, a politician scolded Chesterton for resisting reform in the same way Mesopotamian priests likely defied the development of the wheel. "I pointed out, in reply, that it was far more likely that the ancient priest made the discovery of the wheels. It is overwhelmingly probable that the ancient priest had a great deal to do with the discovery of writing."

Whereas skeptics claimed Christianity merely subsumed toxic elements from a worn-out paganism, Chesterton depicted the basic pagan instincts—say for the supernatural or the festive—as both sane and human. In the end, Chesterton insisted, Christianity incorporated the best of the ancient world: "It is thoroughly bad history to suppose that it was the Paganism that absorbed the Christianity; when there are a thousand things to show that it was the Christianity that absorbed the Paganism."

But again, if an economic-cultural collapse came tomorrow, in what shape would the Church find herself to respond? In his book, *The Long Emergency*, James Howard Kunstler imagines the Church in this scenario wearing the violent mask of millennially crazed Bible-belt Christians.

As a historian looking back, Chesterton is more hopeful. He notes that in the "dark ages" a return to "simplicity" followed the collapse of western Roman power. Certainly, in a time of crisis, the contemporary Church would need to reconfigure herself more locally—as a place you could jog to. My seminary Church History professor described the European parish system where he grew up, saying "You belonged to the congregation whose steeple you could see from home." During a period of cultural decay, the Church also would have greater opportunities for leadership, education, and service—as when Gregory the Great rebuilt Rome's aqueducts, organized food distribution, raised an army, and negotiated directly with Lombard aggressors. As Chesterton commented in *A Hope for the Decline of Civilization*:

> "Such was the return to simplicity at the beginning of the Dark Ages, of which some people talk as if they were literally and materially in the dark; as if Bede or Dunstan or Gregory the Great went groping about as though they were in a London fog.... Men lived in a much clearer world in the sixth century; in what has been finely called 'that long evening by the Mediterranean.'"

ON TREADMILLS

Technology embodies an unmitigated evil—always the temptation to take the easy way out, always a path toward destruction; and Chesterton would agree, right? "When we say this is the age of the machine," he mused, "that our present peace, progress and universal happiness are due to our all being servants of the machine, we sometimes tend to overlook the quiet and even bashful presence of the machine gun ..." In *The Ball and Cross*, what symbolizes modern machinery at the end of the book is the asylum—with its "cold miracles of modern gunnery."

Currently I'm staying at a Marriott Hotel west of Chicago—near a university housing a collection of Chesterton's correspondence. I'm hoping the Marriott does not sport machine guns on the roof as part of their modern technological safety and "comfort package." Fighting a cold, I tossed and turned most of the night, snuffling and hacking. I rolled out of bed before 6:00 a.m., unusually early for me. Since my wife and daughter were still sleeping, I thought I would go running. I had two options. First, I could run outside, facing a frustrating run: perhaps with sidewalks, but likely not; yet certainly tackling annoying starts and stops every block for traffic, caged at cross-walks by lights and cars, dodging through one more labyrinth of America's "geography of nowhere"—past faceless strip malls, restaurant chains, bank branches, and gas stations. Instead, I opted for the treadmill in the hotel exercise room where the temperature remained a steady 68 degrees, with towels piled neatly next to the water cooler, and Katie Couric chattering away in the background about some aspect of U. S. immigration policy. After a half hour the man next to me dripped away (to his room I hope). I switched off CBS so I could pray for a few minutes. "Technology is okay if it's used properly, right?" As I was having this internal monologue, I recalled Chesterton's opinion of large, impersonal American hotels:

> A fine American epic might be written about the battle in the
> big hotel, with its multitudinous cells for its swarming bees. It
> might describe the exciting battle for the elevators; the war of the

nameless and numberless guests, known only by their numbers. It might describe …. The deathless deeds of 65991, whose name, or rather number, will resound for ever in history.

Of course, in light of the battle of the lamps in *The Napoleon of Notting Hill*, Chesterton's satire is obvious. Who would *not* want to defend Notting Hill with its quaint shops and shopkeepers? But who, on the other hand, would care an ounce about defending Marriott room # 417 in the west Chicago suburbs somewhere off of I-88 between I-294 and I-355? A healthy optimism might dare to declare, "My cosmos right or wrong," but to fight for machines seems rather addled. I understand we're talking about a matter of degree. I might fight for a decent commuter train to Chicago, for more light-rail in Portland, certainly for a good bicycle, but only to the degree that they would help foster in me and others a deeper humanity.

At some point technology does seem to make us less human, doesn't it—relegating people to mere numbers? Never mind that half the time technology fails to even work: "The modern world is a crowd of very rapid racing cars all brought to a standstill and stuck in a block of traffic," Chesterton noted. Surely, if we are talking about treadmills, then yes, we risk become less human, less connected to the world around us and to our own rhythms as they are linked with nature. We could never imagine Chesterton on a treadmill, could we—much to the treadmill's relief, I'm sure. Though perhaps we could consider a new line of G. K. jokes that all began with the question: "What did the treadmill say when Chesterton arrived?"

But our choice lies not simply between treadmills or trails, between hotels or inns. The point is that through our addiction to technology in the West we continue to separate ourselves from nature, from each other, from our very selves, and from God—mirroring, incidentally, the alienating effects of the Fall of human beings in the garden (Genesis 3).

> Comforts that were rare among our forefathers are now multiplied in factories and handed out wholesale; and indeed, nobody nowadays, so long as he is content to go without air, space, quiet, decency and good manners, need be without anything whatever that he wants; or at least a reasonably cheap imitation of it."

It is not that Chesterton is arguing for no technology—for no toasters and no trams.

> Unless the Socialists are frankly ready for a fall in standard violins, telescopes and electric lights, they must somehow create a

moral demand on the individual that he shall keep up his present concentration on these things. It was only by men being in some degree specialist that there ever were any telescopes....

Rather, Chesterton warns that the world should feel "the *danger* of machinery deadening creation, and the value of what it deadens." He sanely proposes "admitting them [machines] for particular purposes, but keeping watch on them in particular ways." Vigilance, then—that key New Testament virtue—ought to serve as the guardian of all our use of technology. Yet how painfully difficult, while plodding on a hotel treadmill, to muster anything at all like vigilance.

TECHNICALLY SPEAKING

The technical side of running can control you if you let it. What to wear, for instance. What about water-resistant running gear versus waterproof—what's the difference? As you might suspect, waterproof material actually prevents water penetrating, whereas a water-resistant shell normally only minimizes moisture absorption. But runners also need to think about moisture "wicking" fabrics, layering for different climates and seasons, and the breathe-ability of their outfit. And that's just scratching the surface of what to wear. Technical running really subdivides into at least two broad categories—first, *techniques* for better running (hydration, carbo-loading, cross-training, injury-management, etc); and second, the available *technology* (hydration packs, nutrition supplements, ankle braces, and gear from top to toe—from sunglasses to the proper fitting shoes).

I have to admit that I appreciate technology when I run. I buy two pair of quality running shoes at a time, alternating pairs with each run to save my knees. In the dead of Michigan winter, I'm grateful for high-tech ski goggles that keep my contacts lenses from freezing to my brain—and for layers of Coolmax, fleece, and Gore-Tex. In summer, I am happy to slug down a Gatorade before I set out for a seven mile run. But what about taking an I-Pod or cell phone on the jog? Or, what's worse, what about using a treadmill while watching the morning news? Where do we draw the line?

It's interesting that Chesterton—as usual—rejects any simple either/or formula. Though some accuse him of being a Luddite, he clearly refused to denounce all technology outright. We could contrast Chesterton with his friend, Father Vincent McNabb who insisted, "all industrialism was moral evil":

> A devout advocate of the simple life, Father McNabb walked everywhere whenever possible, spurning modern forms of transport. He wore homespun robes and even refused to use a typewriter on the grounds that it was machinery. (Joseph Pearce, ***Wisdom and Innocence*** 181).

In *Outline of Sanity*, Chesterton suggested instead that humans might *use* technology (often discussed under the rubric of "machinery"): "I do not think machinery an immoral instrument in itself." The point is what the technology is used *for*. "If possessing a Ford car means rejoicing in a Ford car, it is melancholy enough …. But if possessing a Ford car means rejoicing in a field of corn or clover, in a fresh landscape and a free atmosphere, it may be the beginning of many things…."

Chesterton implies, first, that technology ought to exist only as a means to an end. The Ford car is not an end in itself, but if it serves other humane purposes—like transporting city folk into rural settings—then it may be a good thing. There are cases where the end *does* justify the means. For instance, Chesterton suggested we *use* technology for Distributist ends.

> I also took the example of a general supply of electricity, which might lead to many little workshops having a chance for the first time. I do not claim that all Distributists would agree with me in my decision here; but on the whole I am inclined to decide that we should use these things to break up the hopeless block of concentrated capital and management…

Secondly, Chesterton frequently asks who's in control—our machines or us. Whereas work is produced *with* a tool; work is done *by* a machine, which removes the human quotient. "I am inclined to conclude that it is quite right to use the existing machines in so far as they do create a psychology that can despise machines; but not if they create a psychology that respects them…." The test becomes both whether we can live without our technology, and whether we can keep from being duped by it. Are we addicted to it? Can we denounce it when necessary? Do we use it, or does it use us—who is master? Saint Paul's dictum comes to mind: all things are permissible, but I will not be mastered by anything. Could we still run in winter without *Under Armour* and in summer without *Dri-Fit*?

Modern advances in medicine, communications, and transportation seem nearly miraculous at times. But if technology fosters in us a sense of prowess, it also tempts us toward idolatrous hubris. Do we as moderns grin so uncritically at our "advances" that we never pause to consider our goal? In the end, Chesterton avows there is only one legitimate purpose for technology—to make us better humans. "We are concerned to produce a particular sort of men, the sort of men who will not worship machines even if they use machines."

I don't think Chesterton would have let technology control him. "None of the modern machines," he insisted, "none of the modern paraphernalia ...have any power except over the people who choose to use them." Yet I could imagine him appreciating sane technology. Were he alive today, I would *not* expect him to hurry out and buy all the latest running "gear and tackle and trim." But I can imagine him picking up a pair of state-of-the-art walking shoes and marveling at a good Gore-Tex shell—for the purpose, that is, of taking long country walks in the dreariest of weather.

THE POETRY OF LAMP-POSTS

One might consider jogging as a merely rural, bucolic pastime, but I think Chesterton would argue just as adamantly for urban jogging. In fact, Chesterton sometimes champions civilization over nature—the clearest case appearing in a poem titled simply *The Lamp Post* (which can be compared with an earlier, untitled version). Let me emphasize two points. First, Chesterton paints nature with a cruel face. The opening line reads, "Laugh your best, O blazoned forests...." Two stanzas later, we realize the forest's laugh is not a merry one, with the line: "Laugh ye, cruel as the morning...." Compare the opening stanza of the earlier version:

> And the Woods, with gnarled and cruel
> Hoary humor of the earth
> Cry as at a barren Woman
> Evil jests of death and birth

I don't know about the neighborhood you jog in, but where I jog we do not consider crying at barren women good manners. Or how about the sinister sound of stanza four from *The Lamp Post*:

> We have read your evil stories
> We have heard the tiny yell
> Through the voiceless conflagration
> Of your green and shining hell.

Chesterton evokes a rather chilling air.

Second, contrast this depiction of nature as cruel and pitiless with the role of the lamp-post in the poem as an ensign of civilization:

> Laugh your best, O blazoned forests,
> Me ye shall not shift or shame
> With your beauty: here among you
> Man hath set his spear of flame

That "spear of flame" is the lamp-post. And it sounds like preparations for war are materializing.

Lamp to lamp we send the signal,
For our lord goes forth to war;
Since a voice, ere stars were builded
Bade him colonize a star.

A notebook entry written about the same time corroborates the magnitude of the conflict between nature and civilization: "I remained a considerable time staring at one particular lamp-post. Even an ordinary lamp-post is indeed a thing at which poets might gaze longer than at a primrose, for it is the ensign of man's war upon Old Night with fire, his stolen star." Our friend the lamppost thus stands straight as the Promethean defender of civilization (and of civilized jogging, I might add).

Notice how the lamp-post symbolizes for Chesterton—humanity forged in the image of God. We have been trusted with a divine mandate as co-creators: "Since a voice, ere stars were builded/ Bade him colonize a star." We have colonized cities; we have domesticated animals; we have built jogging paths—and the lamp signifies God's gift to us of creative imagination. A line from an *Illustrated London News* article reads: "the lamp-post really has the whole poetry of man, for no other creature can lift a flame so high or guard it so well." Lamp-posts represent the lofty place God has awarded us in the scheme of creation: "What are human beings that you spare a thought for them, or the child of Adam that you care for him? Yet you have made him little less than a god..." (Psalm 8:4-5).

Our friend the lamp-post—as ensign of civilization—figures prominently in another 1890s poem, *Modern Elfland*. The narrator begins the poem with preparations for entering fairyland, carrying all the necessary talismans—including a feather in his cap from an angel's wing and a wallet filled with white stones (perhaps as sling ammunition against a giant). Having thus fortified himself, he tells us, "And so I went to fairyland." But when he arrives, he discovers that "science" (as in "science and industry") has already arrived as aggressor. Chesterton is referring to the industrial revolution with its soot spewing factories and "iron crown" of the coal burning locomotive—signs of war "that telleth where she (science) takes a town." Indeed, a battle with leviathan is brewing: "Like sleeping dragon's sudden eyes/ The signals leered along the line." Even the crooked chimneys "Were fingers signaling the sky." The poet has entered hostile territory. But for all this seeming threat, Chesterton still intuits something redemptive: "Through all the noises of a town/ I hear the heart of fairyland." Chesterton discerns that fairyland lives and breathes even beneath the layers of soot and noise that so bothered Gerard Manley Hopkins, where all was "seared with trade; bleared, smeared with toil, and wears man's smudge and shares man's smell." In the midst of this martial assault of industry against nature, of materialism against the spiritual standards of Elfland, the following stanza emerges as the interpretive key to the poem:

> But cowled with smoke and starred with lamps,
>   That strange land's light was still its own;
> The word that witched the woods and hills
>   Spoke in the iron and the stone.

Once more, the lamp-light, here, symbolizes everything good within civilization. Smoke hangs in the air, true, but the lamps blaze like stars—placed in the town with pattern and purpose. The light issuing from these gaslight lamps is not something inhuman or foreign to the landscape as we jog past at night. "That strange land's light was still its own." In fact, an affinity exists between the light and the place, a kinship. Moreover, the same Spirit that brings into being this strangely lighted land also "witches" the "wood and hills." So if we marvel at waterfall and rolling hill, shouldn't we also jog gratefully over stone bridges and under iron lamp-posts?

Out of a Nightmare

"Go running; are you kidding?" my friend reacted. "I'd rather flagellate myself with a frayed jogging shoe." People I meet often associate running with pain—as though it's the latest form of torture. Just yesterday a woman passed my wife and me on a vacation jogging path and panted, "I'm still wondering when this is going to start being fun." Maybe a pessimistic view of running surfaces from our worst nightmares where, as some faceless menacing monster pursues us, we run for our lives in terror. (In my nightmares, I confess I run more from a fear of failure—missing a plane or a deadline—than from any grinning fiend).

Earlier this week I experienced the most delightful sort of dreadful dream scenario—one where I not only escaped neatly from danger, but where I returned home successfully from adventure in another world. Hours later I was reminded of the escape in the last chapters of *The Silver Chair* where Scrubb and Jill free Prince Rillian from subterranean captivity. In my dream, it seemed the entire boggy population of this "other world" was chasing us—the "us" consisting of an indistinct version of my wife, daughter, and me; and perhaps a few of our closest friends and loyal servants (though we don't really have servants). It appeared we arrived too late at the entrance to our own world, out of breath and facing a horde of menacing figures. It appeared we had run out of time. But just then a band of that strange land's militia recognized our cause was just and turned to hold the bridge against the malevolent onslaught—in order to "buy us time." The chase was chilling, but now we faced a yawning chasm before us. How could we forge this vast fissure between worlds? How could we get back home? I don't know who among us reacted so quickly or plucked up the courage to scale the giant, Gobble-Fork, but someone mounted his neck as if perched on a steed. Thus, holding tufts of his hair as reigns, our hero whispered in the ogre's ear, beguiling him to stretch over the ravine to our world serving as a bridge. From nowhere a path forward emerged. What none of us knew at the time but our hero, was that if the giant's ear lobe were grasped Gobble-Fork would turn to stone. Imagine our amazement at our fortune: defended from behind by sturdy warriors—foreigners who suddenly understood us—and a magic bridge in front of us leading home.

Yet you may fear that behind us the bridge would soon be overrun by our enemies and that with the giant now transformed into a sandstone stairway hordes of demons might now fly over him in pursuit of us into our world. I don't recall this as part of the dream, but as permissive narrator let me suggest that the hero of our story understood magic. He knew that releasing his grasp on the giant's ear would re-awaken him, so he let go and flung himself headlong into our world while the groggy giant woke, started, and tumbled into the abyss. Being even briefly in that other world of sinister shadow made returning to this world a wonderful homecoming. It was a good day to awaken.

In *The Riddle of the Ivy*, Chesterton tells a friend in Battersea (his home town) that he is traveling to Battersea by way of several countries on the continent. His friend pointed out that he was already in Battersea. But Chesterton insisted there was only one way to find Battersea: "I am going to wander over the whole world until once more I find Battersea." Why must we leave home to find it? In Chesterton's words, "I cannot see any Battersea here; I cannot see any London or any England; I cannot see that door. I cannot see that chair: because a cloud of sleep and custom has come across my eyes." Blindness prevents us from seeing home. Routine puts us to sleep. "The only way to get back [home]," says Chesterton, "is to go somewhere else...."

AT THE MOVIES

One of my favorite issues of **Gilbert** Magazine is the annual film review number. Since film stands as one of our culture's most powerful mediums, it's a good thing when contemporary Christian critics carefully evaluate the worldview assumptions churned out by Hollywood.

It's not easy, however, to compile a list of classic films about sports, let alone about jogging. We might easily identify a great athletic scene—like Roy Hobbs's (Robert Redford's) home run in *The Natural*—or point out a first-rate film here and there—like *Rocky I*, or *Hoosiers*, or more recently, *Glory Road*. But more often than not so-called sports films only exploit a sport as a backdrop for some other theme. Thus, *Bend It Like Beckham* sentimentalizes more about cultural assimilation than about soccer, and the actual soccer scenes in the film come off like a home video of a playground Kung Fu scuffle. *Glory Road* serves as an excellent example of a new level of sports film that not only conveys deep truth, but actually gets the performance of the sport right. An earlier example of a sports film that gets it right—a classic in its own right and probably the best film ever on running—is *Chariots of Fire*.

You remember the plot: Eric Liddle, the fleet of foot Scottish missionary will run against Harold Abrahams, a tenacious Jewish Englishman in the 1924 Olympics. Despite the dated synthesizer music and the agonizingly melodramatic slow-motion running scenes, the movie succeeds in laying out the deeper issues of Abraham's fight against an anti-Semitic British class system that rejects him, and Liddle's struggle to hold religious commitment and culture faithfully in tension. The film ably explores themes of natural ability and inner resources, ambition, pride, and courage—contrasting the different motives Liddle and Abrahams have for running. The movie inspires. Recall, for instance, its most famous line, where Liddle attempts to convince his overly pious sister that running is not irreligious: "I believe God made me for a purpose, but he also made me fast. And when I run, I feel his pleasure."

I have no trouble imagining Chesterton on the edge of his narrow movie seat with a tub of popcorn; I have even less trouble imagining him penning astute film criticism in the ***Illustrated London News***. It is interesting to pose the further question, however, of whether Chesterton would have embraced today's media for his own purposes or whether he would have stood firmly against it as an ephemeral fad. In fact, the question is one Chestertonians enjoy asking. Consider whether or not Chesterton would have "gone Hollywood" were he alive today; whether or not a twenty-first-century Chesterton might have used media to extend his message.

Of course, Chesterton was not completely against media. We know, for instance, that he gave BBC radio talks, and that once he even played a brief part as a cowboy in a silent movie alongside George Bernard Shaw for a benefit. We could imagine him today at least appearing on Letterman or Jon Stewart's Daily Show, if not having his own weekly on EWTN.

But Chesterton worried about several aspects of media—especially when if comes to film as entertainment—that should still concern us today. First, he knew that media easily manipulates. He also knew that commercial interests were as capable of lobotomizing the public as were politicians.

> The cinema is a machine for unrolling certain regular patterns called pictures.... The gramophone is a machine for recording such tunes as certain shops and organizations choose to sell. The wireless is better; but even that is marked by the modern mark of all three; the impotence of the receptive party. ...It is all a central mechanism giving out to men exactly what their masters think they should have.

A friend of mine showed part of a *Simpsons* episode to his class last year to make a point—asking the class in advance to analyze the clip. It astounded him to discover a group incapable of critiquing what they watched. They had been so thoroughly conditioned to receive media passively, they could barely think for themselves when asked.

More and more we simply gape. We wear sports gear like we want to play in the game, but then watch others sweat from our comfortable Lay-Z-Boy. The real world, cries Chesterton, is a "much more beautiful, wonderful, amusing and astonishing thing than any of the stale stories of jingling jazz tunes turned out by the machines. When men no longer feel that [it] is so, they have lost the appreciation of primary things, and therefore all sense of proportion about the world." One of the greatest things about running is that it's a primary thing. It's literally "an elemental" thing—an action that forces us as creatures of nature into nature, into the elements. "The child who can see the pictures in the fire will need less to see the pictures on the film."

We proclaim that we are liberated, free to watch what we want, but Chesterton knew we were becoming more imprisoned. "People who love mechanical pleasures, to such a miracle [as life], are jaded and enslaved." So, after the popcorn and movie, let's go for a run.

LINCOLN

If one were to jog around historical battlefields (hypothetically), then Valley Forge recalls George Washington, Little Big Horn brings to mind Custer, Agincourt evokes Henry V, Waterloo represents Wellington, and Fredericksburg and Chancellorsville signify Lee. But Gettysburg means Lincoln—not a military figure, but a paradoxical politician. The main reason we associate Gettysburg with Lincoln begins with the lines "Four score and seven years ago our fathers brought forth on this continent a new nation"—with the address he delivered there forever engraved on the soul of our nation.

The deeper reasons for pairing Lincoln and Gettysburg, however, relate to how the battle has come to symbolize the paradoxes, contradictions, and sufferings of the war, the man, and the nation. Gettysburg and Lincoln illustrate a worthy cause won through the use of sometimes-dishonorable means; a truth-telling leader who stretched truth to promote a greater truth for a people; and a decisive statesman tortured by the burden of intolerable choices—all realities communicated through Spielberg's recent film, "Lincoln," and truths well known to G. K. Chesterton.

When the American Chesterton Society held its annual conference in Emittsburg, Maryland, at Mount Saint Mary's University in 2010, I drove the twenty minutes each day to Gettysburg to run through the battlefield. At that point, my understanding of the battle remained sketchy at best. Of course, it's not really possible to "take in" the significance of the battle field in three days of jogging—no matter how often one stops to read plaques, back-tracks, and gapes in stretches of awed silence in front of Little Round Top, the High Water Mark, or Cemetery Ridge—the scene of Picket's Charge.

At that point, I knew Chesterton greatly admired Lincoln, so after the conference I began reading. One of the earlier essays Chesterton wrote in the *Illustrated London News* on Lincoln appeared in 1917 contrasting Lincoln's food blockade against Southern states during the Civil War with Germany's WW I use of U-boats to sink English ships regardless of whether they were transporting war supplies, neutral goods, or non-combatants. The differences lie in Lincoln's conscience. As a hook, Chesterton used the controversy surrounding the then-recent erection of a statue of Lincoln in Parliament Square, London—one that common folk evidently felt made Lincoln look "too common." But Chesterton insisted on upholding Lincoln as a plain man, as a man who, because of his conscience, sided with "the people."

Chesterton's chapter in *What I Saw in America* (1922), entitled "Lincoln and Lost Causes," probably remains his most familiar piece on the sixteenth president, but not his best. Yet even in that short chapter Chesterton offers one of his key paradoxical Lincoln insights; namely, that praising Lincoln as a man of success is praising him for the wrong reason.

In 1926 essay, referring again to the statue in Parliament Square, Chesterton stressed Lincoln's logical mind, as a man who "knew exactly what he thought." And if Lincoln's detractors sometimes depicted him as a crude "ape," while his admirers employed hero rhetoric "as if he were a god," Chesterton insisted that Lincoln "was a little more like a man."

Spielberg's movie features both Lincoln's logic and his complex humanity in a portrait Chesterton would have appreciated. Striking parallels appear between the film's portrait of Lincoln and Chesterton's. Spielberg and screenwriter Tony Kushner show us a human Lincoln—a man with flaws and fears, living out paradoxes; a man conflicted, stooped and shuffling down hallways as if carrying the nation on his back.

As Ann Hornaday wrote in a *Washington Post* review, Lincoln emerges in the film "as a complicated, even contradictory figure: wise and wily, manipulative and melancholy, formidable and vulnerable, warm and abstracted." And yet he also managed to "arrive at the destination he was aiming for in the first place." From monument to man is how Hornaday describes Spielberg's rendition of Lincoln (a Chestertonian kind of statement)

In 1928 Gilbert wrote an essay entitled, "Lincoln in Myth and Reality" where he encouraged readers to "turn from imagining the hero to considering the man." He pointed out that Lincoln acted politically in ways others considered "tricky" (what we'd call "shady").He noted that he dressed shabbily—and that others noticed. He was "famous," Chesterton recalled, "for telling dirty or profane stories." He "made a mess of his own domestic affairs." The movie showed us these glimpses of Lincoln and more.

Parallels between Chesterton's essays and Spielberg's movie might simply mean that both men did their homework—both the writer and the director have their facts straight about Lincoln. But the remarkable similarity of the two biographical sketches shows something more significant. In fact, each "artist" understands intuitively something deep about human nature—about how to see the whole of a person's life as flawed yet, at the same time, fundamentally noble. Divine spirit clothed in clay jars; human fragility summoned to greatness through sacrifice. Lincoln's story is the human story.

An American journalist quarreled with Chesterton in the 1920s for insinuating that Lincoln was not a Man of Success, of Progress, or of the Spirit of the Age. Chesterton insisted that Lincoln "thought for himself" too much to blindly follow the spirit of the age: "God has chosen the failures of the world to confound the successes," reminded Chesterton; but then added that Lincoln looked more like a saint in the end, like "one of the Failures who happen to succeed."

THE QUARREL

Chaim and Hersch studied Talmud together in the Yeshiva Beelshtock as young men. During the War each thought the other had died in the camps. But now, in 1948, they accidentally meet in a park in Montreal— old friends reunited, on Rosh Hashanah of all days. The film *The Quarrel*, an adaptation of Chaim Grade's play, consists chiefly of the argument between these two men: Hersch , an Orthodox rabbi who recently founded a Yeshiva in Montreal, and Chaim who's lost his faith and now earns his living in New York City as an atheist intellectual writer. Hersch insists that life makes no sense without God, but for Chaim, the extent of evil unleashed in the holocaust negates the possibility of God's existence. When it comes to evil and suffering, Hersch allows for mystery: "If I knew God, I'd be God," he exclaims. Chaim retorts bitterly: "If I knew God, I would put him on trial."

Throughout the movie, Hersch and Chaim debate intensely as they pace through deeply wooded but paved park trails. I've jogged through similar parks. And I've seen the movie so many times, I feel as though I've run through those particular park trails. The path itself, the walking and running route, becomes a key symbol in the film not only indicating the journey these two men take, but visually signifying the give-and-take between them as first one leads, then the other; or as the trail turns and tangles, even separating the two at one point. Chaim lives as an artist. He's an independent thinker. At one turn in the path, as the two argue, he takes what he hopes will be a short cut: "All the paths probably lead to the same place," he boasts. But he ends up momentarily lost, alone, confused.

As we move deeper into the park we are drawn deeper into the debate—a debate that Chesterton would have relished, a debate about things he knew really mattered: questions of God, faith, suffering, religious Judaism, tradition, the role of art and passion, to name a few of the movie's prominent themes (all intermingled with the past personal history of these two friends who now disagree).

One wonders who will win "the quarrel." As a person of faith, it is tempting to assume that the Orthodox Hersch lays out the more satisfying arguments. "If there's no Master of the Universe, who's to say Hitler did anything wrong?" he demands. But twice during the film, at the end of a significant round of the quarrel, the sun emerges from behind clouds to illuminate the face of Chaim the atheist—as if to warn the viewer: do not judge matters too hastily; the Rationalist also has reasons of which the heart perceives little. Perhaps neither wins the quarrel in the end. Perhaps they need each other.

Chesterton would have loved the debate (which is really a better term than *quarrel* for what happens in the film); he would have applauded the theological focus. "You cannot evade the issue of God," Chesterton insisted. God relates to everything worth discussing.

In fact, Chesterton loved all good debates. He began his debating career at an early age—against his brother Cecil. He recalled, "My brother and I **argued** for thirty years and we **never** once quarreled." Chesterton's concern, in fact, was that a quarrel might ruin a good argument. Argument seemed to course through Gilbert's veins. Maise Ward recalled a dinner party where late in the evening a friend discovered Chesterton pacing up and down essentially debating himself, the woman he had begun discussing with long since fast asleep on the nearby couch. As his career led him from his essays in *The Debater*, to the Blatchford controversy, through polemics in print, to sharing the debating stage with contemporaries like H. G. Wells and George Bernard Shaw, Chesterton always aimed to play fair.

I once taught at a school where a colleague asked to mentor me. It sounded like a nice idea so we decided to run together. Often during our time jogging we would debate theological issues, disagreeing on key points. Only later did I discover that my "friend" was using our conversations as "evidence" against me in an effort to get me fired. I wish he'd held more of a Chestertonian sense of fair-play when it comes to debate.

At the surface level, *The Quarrel* is about theological-culture wars— and about who wins this argument of competing ideas. But at a deeper level, the movie is about the relationship between Hersch and Chaim: about friendship and forgiveness. At the start we discover how different the two men have become, how widely their two paths have diverged. As the film progresses we learn how each has betrayed the other or let the other down; we begin to see how each has failed his own family, his people, his own dearest convictions. Toward the end of the film, Hersch confesses his "sins" to the atheist Chaim, and says, "I feel so alone." In response, Chaim confesses that he forsook his family in the war; he weeps: "And now there is no grave where I can ask for their forgiveness." The two men need each other to be whole. The movie ends with the narrator describing Joseph's rise to power in Egypt, only second to Pharaoh in all the land. ""But until his brothers came he was alone."

WAKING UP CHRISTMAS MORNING

How wonderful to wake up Christmas morning! I fully agree with Mr. Fezziwig in the movie *Scrooge*, when he sings: "Of all the days in all the year/ That I'm familiar with/ There's only one that's really fun/ December the twenty-fifth." Bells once woke folks Christmas morning—bells peeling, chiming, clanging; bells ringing, rocking, rousing—bells to stir in us chords of joy and to pry open wide the eyes of children. I'm asking Santa Claus to send bells this year.

But nowadays the culture would rather keep us sleepy. I'm reminded of a scene in the film *My Dinner with Andre*, where Andre tells Wally about a friend who diligently works to avoid the "dream state" trance our culture lulls us in to:

> "Roc used to practice certain exercises, like for instance, if he were right-handed, all today he would do everything with his left hand, all day, eating, writing, everything: opening doors, in order to break the habits of living. Because the great danger he felt for him was to fall into a trance, out of habit. He had a whole series of very simple exercises that he had invented, just to keep seeing, feeling, remembering. Because you have to learn now. It didn't use to be necessary, but today you have to learn..." to be awake.

When our souls grow sleepy we forget who we are, thus easily believing the forces around us telling us we are what we buy, what we wear, how we look, or what we do. "We have all forgotten what we really are," reminds Chesterton, and "we forget that we have forgotten."

Forces of commercialism hope to make us forget the uniqueness of Christmas Day by stretching out the "holiday season" into what we've come to experience as Hallowthankmas. This human-generated spending spree begins earlier each year, and only ends sharply when the last package is purchased. The "market" refuses, in fact, to acknowledge the Twelve Days of Christmas as legitimate religious holy days. Whereas economic interests would fill us fat and tuck us in to slothful sleep, however, true religion would strip us bare and stand us naked before

God. That's partly why I go running on Christmas Day, to shake the sleep from my soul.

Christmas aims to convert, to wake us from our slumber; even if that requires stripping us to our shorts and setting us in the cold. Thus, when Scrooge stands converted in the end of "A Christmas Carol," we find him "as merry as a schoolboy" with his window thrown open to the stirring cold sunlight, still dressed in his bedclothes. When Francis experiences conversion, he heaps his garments at his father's feet in front of the bishop. "He went out half-naked in his hair-shirt into the winter woods," recounts Chesterton, "walking the frozen ground between the frosty trees; a man without a father. He was penniless, he was parentless, he was to all appearances without ... a hope in the world; and as he went under the frosty trees, he burst suddenly into song."

Once, a roaming robber slipped into a forest hermitage and demanded the monk's money. The holy man had no possessions, but sent the thief on his puzzled way with all he owned—his clothes. Sitting naked, then, gazing at a gorgeous full moon, he sighed, "I wish I could have given him this beautiful moon, as well." Chesterton knew that human beings couldn't earn a star or deserve a sunset; and St. Francis lived this truth: "Blessed is he who expecteth nothing for he shall enjoy everything."

My Christmas Day run doesn't happen first thing in the morning. Other celebrations take precedent as part of the wake up routine. But whenever I take my run, it does rouse me.

> "December the twenty-fifth m'dears/ December the twenty-fifth/ The dearest [run] in all the year/ December the twenty-fifth!"

Running wakes me, first, to Christmas gratitude. "Children are grateful when Santa Claus puts in their stockings gifts of toys or sweets. Could I not be grateful to Santa Claus," queries Chesterton, "when he put in my stockings the gift of two miraculous legs?" I recognize that a telegram (or text) could be sent to my family: "Man found alive with two legs." Recall Chesterton's "mystical minimum of gratitude": "At the back of our brains ... there was a forgotten blaze or burst of astonishment at our own existence." Experiencing "this run," I have to ask: "Why am I allowed two?"

Next, there are gifts on the trail to receive and open and cherish: "When you're really shipwrecked, you do really find what you want," insists Michael Moon in *Manalive*. "If we were really besieged in this garden we'd find a hundred English birds and English berries we never knew were here." So, I pay attention to the bright red berries still clinging to leafless twigs and to stunning crimson cardinals, all dressed in their Christmas finery and set against a spectacular white canvas of sun-bedazzled snow: "side by side like two strong colors, red and white, like the red and white upon the shield of St. George." Christmas wakes us "to enjoy enjoyment," with everything on the run becoming "a remnant to be stored and held sacred."

For our Christmas Day run always leads us back to our heart's true home, pointing to Him whom we love and adore:

> And at night we win to the ancient inn,
> Where the Child in the frost is furled,
> We follow the feet where all souls meet,
> At the inn at the end of the world.

COME AGAIN, FATHER CHRISTMAS

During Advent and Christmas I like to add one alteration to my winter running garb—I like to wear a Santa hat when I run. Although I've come less and less to envision Chesterton himself as a jogger over the years, I nevertheless think he'd like the idea of joggers creating especially meaningful rituals for themselves, and especially playful ones. "If you do not have mirth," he counseled, "you will certainly have madness." What better time for mirth than Christmas?

Yet I have this fear that our young people, our culture's children, are growing up insanely fast, forgetting too soon how to play and how to imagine. "The true object of all human life is play," insisted Chesterton. Yet we have traded the magic of the Toy Theatre too glibly for the latest line of educational toys from Zainy Brainy. For instance, I worried that my own daughter in her preschool years felt inclined to disbelieve in things she considered unreal (like fairies) or impossible (like magic). I tried in vain to explain that magic simply signified a different name for miracle. I was only too glad, therefore, when at age six she asked her mother and me whether she could believe in Santa. In an effort to demythologize the consumerist Santa, we had always told her that grandfather and I were Santa; we insisted that a serious difference existed between St. Nicholas, who brought gifts to the poor, and the slick media icons peddling everything from American Girl dolls to international armaments.

When our daughter asked permission to believe in Santa, naturally we granted her wish. To make it easier for her, I decided to get a Santa suit and show up Christmas morning in the house. Christmas Eve she sleeps on the living room couch in front of the tree. Very early I crept into the room, bearded and bedecked in red, and cleared my throat to wake her up. She turned with a start, froze, and quickly shut her eyes tight. I drank the milk and ate one of the cookies we had set out. After a few low rumbling "ho, ho, hos," I went out the garage door to stash my costume. As I was coming up from the garage in our tri-level house, my wife was coming down from the bedroom. For years, my daughter insisted she knew it was Santa because, as she assured us, "He went out the garage and just after that you and mom came out of your bedroom; so I know it couldn't have been you." We were delighted to let her belief in Santa grow.

In the future, when the skepticism of our culture lures my daughter and asks me again about Santa Claus, I will take her to three passages in *Tremendous Trifles* and make two points. The first passage is where Chesterton himself met Father Christmas (in a dream) and had the following conversation:

> "You look ill, Father Christmas."
>
> "I am dying," he said.
>
> I did not speak and it was he who spoke again.
>
> "All the new people have left my shop. I cannot understand it. They seem to object to me on such curious and inconsistent sort of grounds, these scientific men, and these innovators. They say that I give people superstitions and make them too visionary; they say I give people sausages and make them too coarse. They say my heavenly parts are too heavenly; they say my earthly parts are too earthly; I don't know what they want I'm sure.... How can one be too good, or too jolly? I don't understand. But I understand one thing well enough. These modern people are living and I am dead."
>
> "You may be dead," I replied. "You ought to know. But as for what they are doing—do not call it living."

I will then make two points about this passage using two further texts—the first, about Chesterton's openness to the mystical and, the second, about the sanity of fairy tales. As Chesterton confessed:

> I for one should never be astonished if the next twist of a street led me to the heart of that maze in which all the mystics are lost. I should not be at all surprised if I turned one corner in Fleet Street and saw a queer-looking window, turned another corner and saw a yet queerer-looking lamp; I should not be surprised if I turned a third corner and found myself in Elfland.

"Darling," I will inculcate, "stay open to Father Christmas and to elves. Nurture in yourself this healthy mysticism where one cannot be too good or too jolly and where the possibility of elves waits behind every lamppost." Then I will read her the last passage:

> Folk-lore means that the soul is sane, but that the universe is wild

and full of marvels. Realism [in modern literature] means that the world is dull and full of routine, but that the soul is sick and screaming. The problem of the fairy tale is—what will a healthy man do with a fantastic world? The problem of the modern novel is—what will a madman do with a dull world?"

"Sweetheart," I will plead, "always remember the healthy, wild, and joyous meaning of the Santa story. It's not Father Christmas who's dying, but our modern world."

I think of my December Santa jogging hat as a way to invite winter elves and fairies to join me on my rural run. This year I am thinking of adding bells to my outfit, and perhaps a sign reading, "Come back, Father Christmas."

RUNNING HOME FOR CHRISTMAS

Is any run during the year more enjoyable than a Christmas run? I hope it's not simply an escapist inclination for me to think so. True, there's an element of athletic exertion involved in an early yuletide jog that helps prepare for the difficult task of feasting later in the day; but that's not the primary reason why I appreciate the run so thoroughly. Yes, there's a sacramental aspect to the simple ritual of running each Christmas Day. Surely part of the joy of a Christmas run has to do with the festivity of the day. You may think I'm joking, but it's especially fun to run on Christmas Day. Naturally, if it snows, all the better—like when it snowed in Switzerland on Christmas Eve 1986, leaving branch and bramble on the trail to Diessenhofen blanketed with six inches of soft whiteness. But even if it doesn't snow, our Michigan landscape ornaments itself with tall spruce, medium-sized juniper, and red-berried underbrush. What more could Father Christmas ask for? Even if the temperature is warm, or if it rains, the houses in town twinkle with colored lights and the telephone poles stretch along Main Street lined with tinseled wreaths and colored bells.

Though the streets appear poignantly vacant, as I get out of town maybe I'll spot Brent Williams taking hay to his cows, or spy Bob Copernoll bringing in firewood—and shout to them a muffled, "Merry Christmas" through layers of running gear. They'll think I'm looney: running in this weather wearing a long Santa hat.

But it's not only fun to get out, it's also fun to peer in—to consider all those warm living rooms and (hopefully) cheerful hearths.

> A child in a foul stable,
> Where the beast feed and foam;
> Only where He was homeless
> Are you and I at home

Christmas creates in us this longing for home. Peering in at the Cratchit's window—poor as they are—Scrooge recognizes the warmth and happiness of home—home not so much as an idea, as a hard won reality.

But why is the Christmas run any different than other holidays—say different than Easter or the Fourth of July? It dawns on me that most of our married life, we have traveled to see family for Christmas. When we were growing up in Portland, Oregon we kids thought the thirteen-hour trip to Los Angeles counted against our sins in purgatory; but in the Midwest, a twelve to fourteen hour drive is often only the first leg of the trip. Smushed into a compact car for two days can make a person pine for a long run on Christmas Day. Consider the plight of an introvert, then, closed in a three bedroom house with nineteen people—no matter how cheery their dispositions. In this scenario, a Christmas Day run appears as a happy chance to steal a few moments of bucolic peace in the midst of an otherwise raucous affair.

I hope it's not that I'm a misanthrope. There are those times, of course, when uncle George appears unannounced. Chesterton comments on the scene: "A Christmas dinner, as described by a modern minor poet, would almost certainly be a study in acute agony: the unendurable dullness of Uncle George; the cacophonous voice of Aunt Adelaide." Chesterton goes on to explain how Chaucer, who knew the commoner well, "could have sat down to a Christmas dinner with the heaviest uncle or the shrillest aunt. He might have been amused at them, but he would never have been angered at them, and certainly he would never have insulted them in irritable little poems." Chesterton cites two reasons for Chaucer's good spiritual manners: first, because he "knew that Christmas was more important than Uncle George's anecdotes; and [second] because he had seen the great world of human beings, and knew that wherever a man wanders among men…, he will find that the world largely consists of Uncle Georges." The desire to escape the Uncle Georges of the world on Christmas Day by running requires restraint. The problem is not that Uncle George is so obnoxious, really, but that I am so small-minded. Chesterton's Christmas advice to me this year comes through these lines from **Orthodoxy**:

> How much larger your life would be if your self could become
> smaller in it; if you could really look at other men with common
> curiosity and pleasure; if you could see them walking as they are
> in their sunny selfishness and their virile indifference! You would
> begin to be interested in them, because they were not interested
> in you. You would break out of this tiny and tawdry theatre in
> which your own little plot is always played, and you would find
> yourself under a freer sky, in a street full of splendid strangers.

May our homes this Christmas grow in true hospitality; into places where others begin to long for their true home:

> To an open house in the evening
> Home shall men come,
> To an older place than Eden
> And a taller town than Rome.
> To the end of the way of the wandering star,
> To the things that cannot be and that are,
> To the place where God was homeless
> And all men are at home.
> (*The House of Christmas*)

The Distributist Santa

As I jog during December, I frequently notice life size Santas perched on porches or lounging in yards. But the singular form in which they appear disappoints me: always the dimpled doting oversized cherub; never the distinguished, jollified Father Christmas. It is not that I doubt the real Santa's existence. Rather, I question the motives of the impostors.

Though Chesterton believed in a real Santa Claus, he nevertheless was broadminded about his Christmas dogmas: "Personally, of course, I believe in Santa Claus; but it is the season of forgiveness, and I will forgive others for not doing so." He situated belief in Santa in that category theologians label "things indifferent"—"all that fringe of mere fancy that is attached to faith, and yet is detachable from it."

Yet G. K. would surely distinguish between the compelling figure of Father Christmas and the current Santa heresy promoted by North American commercialism. I for one do not want to encourage any easy acceptance of capitalism's consumerist Santa. I recall only too well the Dickensian story Gracie Seavers told me. Gracie, a shut-in in my first church, had lived her whole life in this one-horse, one-church town. Somehow the tiny berg developed the odd Christmas tradition of having "Santa" ride into town on a local fire truck with a bag full of toys purchased by parents and then distributed by this counterfeit Santa in the church basement. "I thought Santa was a cruel and wicked man," Gracie confided. "Goodness, why?" I asked. "Well, you see, when he opened his sack every year, he gave the best presents to all the meanest, proudest, naughtiest children. My parents were poor, so all I got each year was an orange. How glad I was," she recalled with a glimmer, "when I was finally told that Santa Claus was not real; then I could enjoy the orange given to me for the gift it was." Some Santas, it appears, should be disbelieved in. This makes me think that a Chestertonian, Distributist version of Santa ought to be offered our culture. Chesterton might have put it this way: If Santa is a bad thing, nobody should have him; if Santa is a good thing, he somehow belongs to everyone.

A few months ago I visited Estes Park, Colorado, a touristy town in Rocky Mountain National Park lined with trinket shops, restaurants, and candy stores. It rained heavy and steadily all day. We had taken refuge in an Italian restaurant for dinner and were enjoying watching the crowds pass by from our window seat. As I gazed up at the peaks, I noticed the faces of the children (some of them obviously from poorer families) staring in the window as they passed in the pouring rain. I was warm on the inside. They were on the outside looking in—like Pip in Great Expectations.

This made me think that a Distributist Santa might look very Dickensian to Chesterton. Two sides of the face of this robust red fellow would smile out at us—jolly Father Christmas on one side, and pious St. Nicholas on the other. "In fighting for Christmas," G. K. claimed of Dickens, "he was fighting for the old European festival, Pagan and Christian, for that trinity of eating, drinking and praying ..., for the holy day which is really a holiday." Here, all the merriment and joy expressed by Scrooge's second ghost flows forth—that "jolly Giant, glorious to see," lounging upon his feast-laden couch with glowing torch. Father Christmas comes to spread comfort. "The forms and rites of Christmas Day are meant merely to give the last push to people who are afraid to be festive. Father Christmas exists to haul us out of bed and make us partake of meals too beautiful to be called breakfasts."

The other side of Santa's face ought to show the visage of St. Nicholas, whose special concern is to spread comfort and mirth to the poor (the matter, as Chesterton insists, "of spending large sums on small feasts"). Charity must be wary of condescension at this point. G. K. agreed with Dickens that the rich had precious little to teach the poor about Christmas happiness.

> He [Dickens] fell furious on all their ideas [those of the rich]: the cheap advice to live cheaply, the base advice to live basely, above all, the preposterous primary assumption that the rich are to advise the poor and not the poor the rich."

It certainly is not the size of the yuletide feast that counts. "The merry-maker wants a pleasant parlour, he would not give twopence for a pleasant continent." What a Christmas feast really desires, argues Chesterton, is coziness; just that kind of coziness we experience as we stare in the window from the cold at the Cratchit Christmas feast.

> There was nothing of high mark in this. They were not a handsome family; they were not well dressed; their shoes were

far from being waterproof; their clothes were scanty…. But they were happy, grateful, pleased with one another, and contented with the time; and when they faded, and looked happier yet in the bright sprinklings of the Spirit's torch at parting, Scrooge had his eye upon them, and especially on Tiny Tim, until the last.

Father Christmas might teach us to find real joy in what we have this year; St. Nicholas might show us ways to share what we have with others. I'm still scanning everywhere I run—in yards and on porches—for one of these two true Christmas figures to appear.

THE DONKEY

When I run solo, my main route takes me out of town, south on Teft Road, past the Williams' Dairy Farm (Est. 1914). On the east side of Teft lies the farm proper with its long low cow sheds, adjacent feed barn, and the open gravel lot allowing for the constant flow of John Deere tractors, red corn wagons, and pick-up trucks. On the west side sits Brent's house and a corral fencing four small horses—at least I always assumed they were horses as I ran by. But the other day I was talking to a friend who remarked: "Doesn't one of those horses look like a donkey? Its ears are so long." It's true. I haven't yet climbed the fence to measure its ears, but they do seem to reach out to heaven like a dancing child's arms.

Whenever I see a donkey, I'm reminded of Chesterton's famous poem by that title. On receiving a copy of *Wild Knight* from Chesterton's publisher, Rudyard Kipling replied, "Of course I knew some of the poems before, notably *The Donkey* which struck in my mind at the time I read it." The radical combination of grotesque images of a donkey with Christ's passion makes the poem arrestingly memorable; thus serving as a fitting Lenten meditation.

Stanza one needs to be interpreted as a whole, but I confess, I have little idea what it really means: "When fishes flew and forests walked/ And figs grew upon thorn/ Some moment when the moon was blood/ Then surely I was born." As far as I can discern, fish seldom fly and forests rarely walk. Chesterton certainly is not referring to some evolutionary epoch on earth—when fishes flew—but rather to a topsy-turvy eschatological moment when things were turned upside down and all creation hung breathless in the balance. A clue sounds in the next stanza: "With monstrous head and sickening cry/ And ears like errant wings/ The devil's walking parody/ On all four-footed things." With the devil's entrance, we are assured that some major spiritual struggle for the souls of human beings is afoot.

Perhaps the entire poem echoes the Passion of Christ (whether or not Chesterton intended this is another question). The moon turning to blood was prophesied in Joel chapter two and, according to Peter (in Acts chapter two) this prophecy was fulfilled in the death and resurrection of Christ (when the sun turned to ash at midday during the Crucifixion). What if the "monstrous head" and "ears like errant wings" symbolize the disfigured Christ, slumped slightly with bloody split lip and swollen eye as Pilate presented him to the crowd: "he has no form or comeliness; and when we see him there is no beauty that we should desire him?" (Isaiah 53:2) "Behold, the man!" scoffs Pilate. If this reading has merit, then no wonder the devil mocks in parody.

The "sickening" cry ringing forth recalls the deep soul suffering Christ experienced on the cross and his final lament to his Father: "My God, my God, why have you forsaken me?" Earlier, then, the "thorn" in line two ("And figs grew upon thorn") conjures up Christ's contemptuous crown and perhaps also his flogging. Conceivably this explains why Lent falls for us in the West at the end of winter where in northern climes like Michigan, brown brambles waiting to bud and twisted thickets clutching red berries point to the piercing of our Lord.

Next, we find a stanza, however, where this interpretation of the poem may falter: "The tattered outlaw of the earth/Of ancient crooked will." "Tattered outlaw"—yes!—Christ was executed by Rome as a common criminal, bartered by the public for the insurrectionist Barabbas and crucified between two malefactors. But how could "Of ancient crooked will" ever describe Christ? This apparent non sequitor implies the humanity of Christ adopted through his Incarnation as the Second Adam. Not that his will revealed any crookedness, but on the cross he took all that bent history of our race upon himself for our salvation.

The next string of images returns more plainly to the Passion: "starve, scourge, deride me, I am dumb, I keep my secret still." Except for "starve," the rest of the line reads like a sequencing of the Passion narrative: "scourge" (Pilate failed to appease the irate mob); "deride" ("the passers-by jeered at him....Even the bandits who were crucified with him taunted him in the same way" (Matthew 27:39, 44). The next line—"I am dumb, I keep my secret still"—refers not only to the silence of non-retaliation, as in "yet when he was afflicted he didn't open his mouth" (Isaiah 53:7), but also to Jesus' hesitancy to subscribe to the then-current Messianic expectations (what we would call "the Messianic Secret").

The poem closes dramatically with a challenge for us all: "Fools!" cries the donkey, "for I also had my hour,/ One far fierce hour and sweet/ There was a shout about my ears/ And palms before my feet." Our donkey thus functions as herald offering a choice: we can either live as fools, declaring there is no God (cf. Psalm 14:1), or we can peer through the disfigured Jesus to discover Christ the Savior. Interestingly enough, the opposite of a fool is not necessarily an intelligent person, but rather one humble enough to see God—like the Donkey, or like Chesterton himself (whose own head sometimes appeared a bit "monstrous").

The Essential Mystery

Good Friday appears as an Essential Mystery. I don't mean, "It's essentially a mystery," I mean it's an *essential mystery*—in contrast to an *accidental mystery*. The distinction between essential mystery and accidental mystery represents one of those theological classifications professors come up with to help explain the indescribable. An accidental mystery becomes clearer when the mystery is solved. So, in the case of a murder, when you discover Col. Mustard perpetrated it, in the kitchen, with the candlestick, everything becomes clear. This is true of Father Brown mysteries. We discover that the Presbyterian blacksmith was not connected to the "hammer murder" of Colonel Bohun, but instead his own cleric brother, Wilfred, let the hammer fall from the church belfry as a judgment from God: case closed, mystery solved. Many of my friends consider my jogging a mystery, but it's merely an accidental mystery. Once I explain where I jog and why, it all makes exquisite sense (except to the Chesterton Society's beloved Dale Ahlquist for some paradoxical reason).

In contrast, when one attempts to answer an essential mystery, the mystery only deepens. Essential mystery includes all the Church's most cherished doctrines. Question: What is the Incarnation? Answer: the infinite God entered time and became human. Question: How are we to understand the Person of Christ? Answer: Jesus was both fully human and fully God. Often these essential mysteries come paradoxically packaged—as in Virgin Birth, or Three-in-One God, or Good Friday—as if it made complete sense to speak of a Divine Death or a Crucified God.

I used to teach a seminary class on Church History where I would give an assignment in Early Church Christology. The assignment first forced students to diminish either Jesus' humanity or divinity. It's an obvious false choice, but if forced which would you choose to diminish? Which emerges as most crucial for you to keep? Then Part Two of the assignment asked students to explain why both humanity and divinity are necessary in the person of Christ. What's interesting is that about 95% of younger students choose to diminish Christ's divinity. Earlier Ages would have answered this differently, I'm sure.

Theologian Paul Tillich sketched three periods of anxiety in human history: ancient, medieval, and modern. In the ancient Hellenistic world, people generally believed in human goodness, but they weren't so sure of eternity. They would easily have understood the line of the hymn that runs, "Time like an ever rolling stream bears all her sons away," or the Icelandic myth that laments: "Baldir the beautiful is dead, is dead." Life is good, but too short and too precarious. The joy of running, we might note, is counterbalanced by the tragedy of human frailty and finitude where joints deteriorate and cartilage tears. In contrast, medieval folk were convinced of the afterlife, but were obsessed with human sin in the face of a holy God. Human infirmity so often appears like judgment—or at least plague affords opportunity for purgation. One might imagine a good medieval ascetic running a marathon instead of fasting or in lieu of wearing a hair shirt. But the modern person worries about meaninglessness, claimed Tillich. Running is stupid. We are lost in the cosmos; lost on the run—alone; courageous perhaps, but frail as a reed in a storm.

Both ancients and medieval citizens would have opted for a divine rather than a human Christ, for they knew they needed help from beyond the merely human. When it comes to Good Friday, they would have agreed with Chesterton that "It does not especially humanize the universe to say that good and wise men can die for their opinions; any more than it would be any sort of uproariously popular news in an army that good soldiers may easily get killed."

But contemporary people want a Jesus they can identify with: tempted in every way as we are, yet without sin; a high priest not unable to sympathize with us. Protestant Pietism, in fact, comes to the foot of the cross like this: to gaze on the human sufferings of Jesus, where the clinical details of Jesus' sufferings are rehearsed painstakingly and magnified minutely, from scourging, to the size of the nails, to the medical reasons given for Our Lord's labored breathing on the cross. We see this same tendency in Gibson's *The Passion of the Christ*—which ironically mirrors the Good Friday mindset of Protestant Pietism.

I don't want to sound impious, but death by crucifixion is NOT the most painful human death. There are more painful ways to suffer—and countless human beings have experienced worse pain, for much longer durations, than Christ did on the cross.

My point is to stress that our Redemption, our Atonement, is NOT somehow dependent on how much Christ suffered physically on the Cross—as if increase in his pain wins us more forgiveness. It is important to realize that Christ's greatest suffering, in fact, took place within the supernatural realm, inaccessible to human eyes. As Chesterton avers in **Orthodoxy**:

> "When the world shook and the sun was wiped out of heaven, it was not at the crucifixion, but at the cry from the cross; the cry which confessed that God was forsaken of God.... Nay (the matter grows too difficult for human speech), but let the atheists themselves choose a god. They will only find one divinity who ever uttered their isolation; only one religion in which God seemed for an instant to be an atheist.

The fact is, within the Gospels themselves, there is little lingering around the human suffering of Jesus and much more emphasis on Good Friday as a supernatural event within the realm of the divine: darkness, earthquake, the temple curtain sundered.... As I contemplate the essential mystery of our faith this Lent, as I run amidst the still barren landscape of south central Michigan, there is probably no better response than to wonder at the mystery in silence.

REVELRIES IN THE RAIN

I recall mist rain runs on fog-shrouded beaches and dapple-dripping runs through moss-bearded tree trails where the spongy peat path put a spring in one's step. But not every rainy run is a fun run. When slanting twenty-five mile per hour water missiles burst squarely against your face, loaded with brain-numbing wind chill; when cartilage-chilling cold seeps past all protective layering and fills each shoe to twelve pounds—an inner conversation ensues about buying a basement treadmill where you can exercise and watch the *Apostle of Common Sense* at the same time. It's weather like this that causes one to question the meaning of rain.

Too much rain, of course, can spoil things—ruining crops, commerce, homes, livelihoods, and lives. We shouldn't wax overly romantic about rain. As cheerfully as Chesterton welcomed all sorts of weather, he could nevertheless acknowledge "a dismal night with rain still dropping from the trees ...." He could speak of "ruin and the rain that burns." If nature is our mother, he noted in **Orthodoxy**, then she often appears as wicked stepmother. When Remarque wanted to sketch the meaninglessness of trench warfare in *All's Quiet on the Western Front* he used constant rain as the pigment: "monotonously falls the rain. It falls on our heads, it falls on the dead up the line ...; it falls in our hearts."

As a native Portlander (Oregonian), though rain could certainly dampen things, I never knew rain's fierce face until I moved to the Midwest. Then I witnessed the Leviathan that causes "mountains to shake in the heart of the sea" (Ps. 46:2); the monster only Elohim can vanquish: "you broke the heads of the dragons in the waters;" "when the waters saw you, O God ...the very deep trembled" (Psalms 74:13; 77:16). But like England, rain in Portland and Seattle rarely interrupts plans. That's why Chesterton could assert with confidence, "I do not generally agree with those who find rain depressing." No doubt that's because, in England (as in the Northwest), "rain is not so much an incident as an atmosphere." A romantic tinge to Chesterton's thoughts on rain is therefore excusable, though he never merely observes rain from a safe indoor shelter. In an undated but early letter to a friend, he wrote:

> I have just been out and got soaking and dripping wet; one of my favorite dissipations. I never enjoy weather so much as when it is driving, drenching, rattling, washing rain....Seldom have I enjoyed a walk so much. My sister water was all there and most affectionate. Everything I passed was lovely... the gutters boiling like rivers and the hedges glittering with rain. And when I came to our corner the shower was over, and there was a great watery sunset right over No. 80, what Mr. Ruskin calls an 'opening into Eternity.'.... Yes, I like rain. It means something, I am not sure what; something refreshing, cleaning, washing out, taking in hand, not caring-a-damn-what-you-think, doing-its-duty, robust, noisy, moral, wet.

Once when traveling with a friend by train in Belgium—having gotten off for a hike at the wrong stop—it began to pour. The two friends eventually made it back to the station "sodden and dripping." Evidently the rain did not stay "mainly on the plain." Instead, it fell on them suddenly like a wall. And though he admitted he "really did think things a trifle dreary" Chesterton still experienced this strange town rainstorm as an adventure. "If it is exciting when a man throws a pail of water over you, why should it not also be exciting when the gods throw many pails?"

We can understand why Chesterton had little patience with the sort of Western consumerist hedonism that moans about rain ruining weddings, graduations, and picnics; as in "rain, rain, go away, I want to jog on a milder day"—as if all of creation needed to check first with our schedule. In his charming essay, *The Romantic in the Rain*, Chesterton cites numerous reasons for rejoicing over rain—"that inspiring and delightful thing." First, rain purifies, signifying "a cosmic spring-cleaning." Most joggers could use such a cleaning—at least by mile four. Second, as a "public bath," as an impartial, "thoroughly Socialistic institution," rain underscores our common humanity and produces a humbling and humanizing effect. The fact that "it rains on the just and the unjust runner" could mean that both are inconvenienced or that both are invigorated. The same rain could destroy the farm of the rich and the poor person, or water the crops of each. Third, rain brings aesthetic beauty as it turns the landscape into "a world of mirrors." Finally, Chesterton celebrated the pure revelry of rain, where "the trees rave and reel to and fro like drunken giants ...clashing cups." Who needs a summer Water

Park when you can run in the rain?

In the end, though, I think something lies behind Chesterton's appreciation of rain that he never states explicitly—namely, his cosmic optimism; as if exclaiming "my weather, right or wrong." To stand in carping criticism over our daily weather is perhaps answered finally by God's Whirlwind Address to Job: "when God is speaking of snow and hail in the mere catalogue of the physical cosmos, he speaks of them as a treasury that he has laid up...." "Where were we," God might ask, "when the foundations of the rains were stored up?"

EXCEPTION TO THE RULE

Christ is risen! He is risen indeed! Easter breaks in on us like spring and this week every leg of my run is exploding into a blooming garden. "Green bombs of bulbs and seeds were bursting underneath me everywhere," cried Chesterton; "and so, as far as my knowledge went, they had been laid by a conspirator." South Central Michigan parades deep green during this season—where "trees are tall and grasses short as in some crazy tale, where here and there a [lake] is blue beyond the breaking pale." Perhaps I am merely nostalgic because Michigan in spring reminds me of where I grew up in Oregon, of the trails I traversed and trees I climbed. But for some reason, as I run on these mild sunny days, with the tulips flowering and the apple trees budding, I keep thinking about the Garden of Eden in Genesis 3 and the fall of our race. What were Adam and Eve thinking? Weren't all the other trees in that great garden enough?

By eating the forbidden fruit, Eve was of course rejecting God as the one who decides what is good and evil, putting herself in that role instead, grasping for what was previously the prerogative of God alone. She somehow thought herself an exception to the rule, a frame of mind representing the very essence of sin. It's the opposite of Kant's categorical imperative. I want everyone else to abide by the rules; to stop at red lights, and not steal my possessions; but I am an exception. In C. S. Lewis's book, *The Magician's Nephew,* Jadis, the Witch who calls herself Queen, tells Digory and Polly how she destroyed all her people with the Deplorable Word. When Digory responds with disgust, the Witch turns on him in anger and chides condescendingly: "You must learn, child, that what would be wrong for you or for any of the common people is not wrong in a great Queen such as I. The weight of the world is on our shoulders. We must be free from all rules." If we see in this statement the choice of Eve and Adam taken to a hideous extreme, then it is distressing to realize how often it is currently being parroted by postmodern advertising as an attitude we personally ought to adopt. One can almost hear Milton's Satan or Lewis's Screwtape promoting the slogan: "Ignore the rules!"

We must understand, moreover, that obeying God often looks to us at the time like the positively wrong running road to take. Consider Digory again as an example. At the end of *The Magician's Nephew* he is sent by Aslan on an errand to fetch a "magic" apple. When he finally reaches the tree, Digory finds the witch waiting for him, hoping to tempt him into taking the apple for himself. Her first tactic coos: eat the apple and you will live forever. Digory knows well enough not to trust her. But then she turns to a kind of deceit that hopes to make evil out of good. "Why not take it for your sick mother, fool," she urges. "Think what she would feel, if she knew you had the chance to save her, but wouldn't!" The witch is hoping to set in motion the same sort of qualifications and questions the serpent presented to Eve. "Did God say you shall not eat from any tree in the garden?" Satan tempted Jesus in the wilderness using a similar ploy. Each of the three temptations in Matthew chapter four can easily be interpreted as an invitation for Jesus to use his Messianic status and power for some benevolent, though limited, human good. According to this line of reasoning, "Turn these stones into bread" means "Feed the hungry masses." "Dive off the temple top and ask angels to catch you" means "Help the masses adopt faith in you and in your God." "Take for yourself all the power of the world's kingdoms" means "Bring peace, justice, and political stability to Israel like no human king ever could." Just as with Eve, the temptation is to think one knows how to run things better than God. One usurps God's role as God.

So what appears to be so life affirming in the beginning of temptation ends up with total self-destruction: those who try to cling to their lives lose them. We think that saying yes to the forbidden fruit promises joy, but it only brings wretchedness. Aslan explains to Digory that, although the witch ate one of the enchanted apples, and so shall have "endless days like a goddess," she has only won for herself "length of misery." If Digory had given the fruit to his mother, she would have revived only to live a life of wretched torment. "That is what happens to those who pluck and eat fruits at the wrong time and in the wrong way," whispered Aslan. "The fruit is good, but they loathe it ever after."

Don't you imagine that when Christ was tempted the second time, in the garden of Gethsemane, the whole universe tilted and tottered on the brink of annihilation? His question echoed nervously, "Father, can this cup pass from me?" What would have happened if he had answered in a convenient way instead of replying as he did, "Thy will be done?"

In the garden of Gethsemane Christ began the reversal of sin and death that Eve and Adam had unleashed in their garden. He asks us each year, through Easter, to enlist in this battle through his Church.

Barns and Noble

One of the things I hold in common with Chesterton is my failure to become an artist. As a child I loved to draw. Mostly I cartooned. Though never nearly as good as Chesterton, I caricatured some, too; but I always wanted to draw realistically. As a college freshman majoring in art, I finally realized I was no good. In my first drawing class, I recall a student who drew a bicycle that looked better than a photograph. "How long have you been drawing," I asked timidly. "Oh, just a few months," she replied with a shy grin. My heart deflated. I wanted to crawl under my desk.

Nevertheless, I recall that the following summer, after I had changed majors, I attempted to sketch a series of barns outside Forest Grove, Oregon—sunburned burgundy and russet barns set against the luminous gold of July crops. Luckily none of those sketches survived.

Back then, I perceived something romantic in barns and as I jog in rural settings today I still do. Old wood barns reveal individuality: often made of local materials, a barn's design depends on the shape of the land, the precise purpose for the barn's use, and the ingenuity of the farmer who designed it. Michigan barns often rest on rings of grouted glacial rock.

I know, of course, that wood barns require constant maintenance—painting and repair. As Chesterton said of fences, if you want a fence to stay white, you have to constantly touch it up. I know we also need good reasons for keeping old barns mended—hay to store; cows to shelter; tractors and tools to guard against the elements. It's distressing to me, therefore, to have witnessed three beautiful barns along my running route razed in the last four years. The rapid disappearance of these wizened structures from the landscape portents some great passing. We're witnessing the demise of a deep culture.

During Thanksgiving, for instance, barns point symbolically to Providence. Since barns exist mainly for storing surplus, they indicate at least the potential for a good harvest gathered. You cannot live long near farmers without recognizing that good harvests do not grow automatically or permanently. Corn, for instance, requires just the right amount of rain—not too much, and not too little, and especially at the right times (as the tassels and ears form). As for apples or oranges, an early frost can decimate the crop (as occurred in the last few years to some Michigan fruit farmers). A good harvest represents not only a tremendous amount of human wisdom, ingenuity, and labor, but also blessing from God. The classic wood barn, itself fragile, easily disintegrating in fire or strong winds, reminds us how precariously human beings walk the earth—and how dependent we are on God as Provider.

Sometimes on my run, as I gaze in astonishment at the fecundity of the earth, I'm reminded of Psalm 104—how God pours out his blessings like a jolly grocer tumbling a feast from tub to table. God pours out a cascade of mountains, hills, valleys, fountains, and trees—all populated with marvelous creatures and supplied with food, but making human beings the prime beneficiaries of God's gracious handiwork:

> You make grass to grow for flocks and herds
> and plants to serve mankind;
> That they may bring forth food from the earth,
> and wine to gladden our hearts,
> Oil to make a cheerful countenance,
> and bread to strengthen the heart (vv. 14-16).

What thanksgiving this should inspire in us; what gratitude!

Chesterton, of course, was well known for his gratefulness: "The test of all happiness," he insisted in *Orthodoxy*, "is gratitude." Moreover, gratitude for Chesterton directly relates to a sense of human finitude and dependency. When we fathom the brittleness of the cosmos, we thank God for not dropping it like a crystal bowl. "I do not, in my personal capacity, believe that a baby gets his best physical food by sucking his thumb," Chesterton exclaimed in his *Short History of England*, "nor that a man gets his best moral food by sucking his soul, and denying its dependence on God or other good things. I would maintain that thanks are the highest form of thought; and that gratitude is happiness doubled by wonder." So the Psalmist sings, "O Lord, now manifold are your works!/ in wisdom you have made them all; the earth is full of your creatures." The Psalmist encourages us to acknowledge God as Creator: "All of them look to you/ to give them their food in due season./ You give it to them; they gather it" (into barns, we might add); "you open your hand, they are filled with good things./ You hide your face and they are terrified;/ you take away their breath, and they die and return to their dust" (vv.25, 28-30).

Perhaps then today's brittle, breaking barns can represent for us our own frail frame: "We walk about like a shadow,/ and in vain we are in turmoil;/ we heap up riches (in barns, of course) and cannot tell who will gather them" (Psalm 39:7). A professor of mine once compared our fleeting life to eating a chocolate éclair—to enjoy it, he forewarned, you must consume it. "Life like an ever rolling stream, bears all her éclairs away." Chesterton might reply, "The only way to truly enjoy an éclair is to appreciate it by eating it with gratitude.

GOING OUT AND COMING IN

Humans exist paradoxically as animals that can transcend themselves. Never on my run have I seen a squirrel throw itself in front of a car to save a fellow squirrel, or help an elderly squirrel across the street, or split its store of winter nuts with orphan squirrels. Nor have I seen sandhill cranes fencing or woodchucks jogging for fun. Although subject to creaturely limitations, humans rise above their limitations—both for good and for evil. In biblical terms humans are a mixture of dust and spirit: "and the Lord God formed man of the dust of the ground, and breathed into his nostrils the breath of life" (Genesis 2:7). Some days I start off my run feeling like spirit; usually by the end I'm re-convinced I'm dust.

At the heart of **Orthodoxy** lies a profound diagnosis of our dual human nature. As Chesterton proposes, humans long for adventure, but also crave security (the influences of spirit and dust). If confined to a running route with comfortable climate and incline, we quickly grow restless. Yet if pushed to our limits—lost in ice-blinding snow on alpine heights or stretched across desolate deserts—our hearts turn pale. So we vacillate between boredom and anxiety. I'm sure that squirrels get neither bored nor anxious.

While Schopenhauer and Nietzsche dissected our bifurcated human condition and preached a hopeless despair, Pascal scrutinized the same evidence and deduced faith in a sovereign God as a reasonable solution. Chesterton also knew that the dilemma of duality touched the core of our being. "How can we contrive to be at once astonished at the world," he asked, "and yet at home in it?" If only continually astonished on our run, we'll take up something less alarming, like Rummy; but shelter us safely in a snug cottage and soon we'll want to jog out of our skin. Chesterton understands our "double spiritual need ... for that mixture of the familiar and the unfamiliar," for a blend "of something that is strange with something that is secure," for that ideal balance of "wonder" and "welcome."

If it does not always prove thrilling, running at least stands as an apt emblem of our twin human desires for adventure and stability, for setting out and returning home. Of course running *can* produce thrills. Consider running in a race, or escaping on foot from some minor childhood misdemeanor, or being chased over a fence by the bull in Melvin's field (I wish Melvin would have told me that he moved him).

Although you cannot arrange to be thrilled or astonished while running, it *does* occur frequently. My wife, Kimberly, and I recently have stumbled upon turtles laying eggs, a fawn nursing, and fledgling sandhill cranes. Just this past year at the Chesterton conference, I saw an eagle dive for a fish in the Mississippi, snatch it up, then bobble and drop it back in the river like a shortstop muffing a grounder. Occasionally on a run I stumble into history. When my in-laws lived in the Missouri Ozarks, while running through Roaring River State Park, I came upon "Devil's Kitchen," a natural shelter made from fallen slabs of sandstone that Confederate guerillas operated out of during the Civil War. And once, as my nephews and I ran through mountain trails northwest of Denver, we happened upon an old roofless miner's cabin, then, minutes later, upon an abandoned sluice and exhausted gold mine.

While American suburbs boast some of the dreariest running routes in the world, I don't want to imply that the only adventurous run is a rural run. It's true, most suburban routes are pathetic. Just this summer, for instance, I stayed at a chain hotel in Any-Town USA where the running route literally trapped me in a seven minute paved loop barricaded on two sides by a six-lane freeway and on the other two sides by cyclone factory fences. It would have taken a tank to break out. To paraphrase Chesterton: "his [running route] moves in a perfect but narrow circle," diseased, like a serpent devouring its own tail.

But not all city running lacks astonishment. One year, during the Chesterton Annual Conference in Minneapolis, I booked a nearby hotel to watch World Cup games. I anticipated an anemic running route that would force me to dodge angry motorists, stop every few minutes at cross walks, and plod alongside hideous American strip malls. Instead, after a short jog from the hotel, my path led me into the lovely labyrinth of St. Paul's Como Park—as astonishing a plot of city green space as one might hope for in the Midwest. In contrast to the current mood of cynicism, which constantly scouts the horizon for the next evil to appear, running could represent for us, spiritually, an expectant and adventurous trust in the next approaching good. My hunch is that squirrels only embrace such adventurous expectations in books written by humans.

In the second paragraph of **Orthodoxy**, Chesterton offers a picture that symbolizes running as it addresses our dual human nature: "What could be more delightful than to have in the same few minutes all the fascinating terrors of going abroad with all the human security of coming home again?" Even so, may the God who fashioned humans with both legs and spirit—"watch over your going out and your coming in from this time forth for evermore" (Psalm 121).

WHERE OUGHT I TO BE?

"The Catholic Church carries a sort of map of the mind," counseled G. K. Chesterton in *Why I am a Catholic*, "which looks like the map of a maze, but which is in fact a guide to the maze." Since about 1990 I have collected maps of routes I've run. A file folder in my office contains maps from cities where I've jogged: Seattle and Portland; Denver and Reno; Kansas City and Iowa City; Prague and Schaffhausen, Switzerland. I also save maps from smaller towns or places I've visited: Lake Ozette in the Olympic Peninsula; Breckenridge, Colorado; Roaring River State Park, Missouri; Apalachicola, Florida; the Thousand Islands in the St. Lawrence Seaway; or the neighborhoods around St. Thomas University in St. Paul.

Part of the reason I am attracted to maps, I confess, is that I'm directionally challenged. To put it mildly, without the aid of maps, I easily find myself lost. I am comforted somewhat when I recall that Chesterton, if not directionally challenged, was at least frequently directionally misplaced. I'm considering developing a whole new line of G.K.C. Running Gear, broadcasting the bold logo: "Where Ought I to be?" Once, when I was exploring a new route nearby, I wrongly assumed the roads were laid out in a logical perpendicular pattern, but finally had to ask someone at a house for directions home. It's a good thing I asked. My six-mile run, which already had turned into a ten-mile run, could have easily ended up as an unplanned (un-trained for) marathon. G. K. might have chuckled: "Robert has always lost his way; the problem now is that he has lost his address."

The deeper significance of maps is that human beings are literally creatures "going somewhere," but who often find directions difficult. Those maps we use to negotiate the terrain of life (and the destination of our afterlife) Chesterton called "dogma." Dogma is the teaching of the Church. Chesterton reminds us that the Church has provided us with "a map in which all the blind alleys and bad roads are clearly marked, all the ways that have been shown to be worthless by the best of all evidence: the evidence of those who have gone down them." Whether or not we admit it, we all have a theological map, a worldview—or what theologian Paul Tillich termed our "ultimate concern." The only question is whether or not our map offers an accurate guide. We ought to ask, "Accurate for what?" That is, "where ought we to be?"

Unfortunately more and more people today reject the map offered by the Church. People still want meaning in their lives, but they don't want it from an institution. In his book *The Holy Longing*, Ronald Rolheiser sums up the contemporary mood:

> Typical today is the person who wants faith but not the church, the questions but not the answers, the religious but not the ecclesial, and the truth but not obedience. More and more typical too is the person who understands himself or herself as a 'recovering Christian,' as someone whose present quest for God has embittered him or her toward the church where there once was membership.

People also typically perceive rejection of the Church as a move away from the more narrow constraints of dogma toward more liberating expressions of faith.

But maps should communicate helpful laws and limits: don't jog across the train bridge—occasionally, trains still use it; don't jog in bear country, especially if you're very slow; don't jog through Jed Mueller's back forty when he's been drinking—even a bad shot gets lucky with a shotgun sometimes. As Chesterton maintained, this is precisely the objective of Church dogma—to mark "certain roads as leading nowhere or leading to destruction, to a blank wall, or a sheer precipice." We shouldn't be angry about a map promising to lead us from Syracuse to Seattle if it also warns us not to drive straight through Lake Michigan.

In fact, people talk today as if good directions are a burden and imposition, as if three limitations out of three million make a dull world. Consider the temptation in the Garden of Eden. Mostly what stands out in our minds is the one veto on the map, the prohibition that affirms: "but of the tree of the knowledge of good and evil you shall not eat" (Genesis 2:17). But with the log of prohibition in our eye, we forget the previous provision: "See, I have given you every plant yielding seed that is upon the face of all the earth, and every tree with seed in its fruit; you shall have all of them for food" (Genesis 1: 29). All trees, all fruit, all roads but one. Perhaps that is what Chesterton had in mind when he muttered, "A man is a fool who complains that he cannot enter Eden by five gates at once."

Often the Church sets herself against worldly fads; but mostly that's because she recognizes how quickly worldly fads fade. For the most part, the Church's map is open—like a jogger's map. The law and limit stands only as an exception. "Catholic doctrine and discipline may be walls," exclaims Chesterton, "but they are the walls of a playground. Christianity is the only frame which has preserved the pleasure of Paganism." Happy trails!

Running Into Heaven

C. S. Lewis once described running as something heavenly. Almost out of nowhere an exhilarating scene appears in the last chapter of the last book of the Chronicles of Narnia. All the heroes and heroines of the story have just entered into heaven through a magical door and have begun moving "further up and further in." The unicorn, Jewel, began to gallop

> which in our world would have carried him out of sight in a few moments. But now a most strange thing happened. Everyone began to run, and they found, to their astonishment, that they could keep up with him: not only the Dogs and the humans but even fat little Puzzle [the donkey] and short-legged Poggin the Dwarf. The air flew in their faces as if they were driving fast in a car without a windscreen. The country flew past as if they were seeing it from the windows of an express train. Faster and faster they raced, but no one got hot or tired or out of breath.

Following this narrative description of "Narnians running deeper into heaven," Lewis comments: "If one could run without getting tired, I don't think one would often want to do anything else." This elevates running to a high level—on par with activities like a sacramental meal with friends, making love, or deep prayer; Lewis describes running as a mystical, heavenly experience.

This is curious because many people I meet consider running as hellish. Returning from a seven-mile run the other day I bumped into a friend in the neighborhood—a real athlete, not a plodding jogger like me. He qualified for the Olympics in the pole vault—and he looks like it. He's a regular muscle man. So he asked me what everyone asks me when they see me drenched with sweat, looking like I'm about to vaporize—"How far did you go today?" "Seven," I replied. In disbelief, as if I'd just endured the torture of crossing the Sahara on one foot, he exclaimed: "That's the farthest I've ever run in my life at one shot." This is not an isolated incident; such conversations occur frequently. Most of my friends, when they discover that I run regularly, quip, "I'm sorry to hear that;" or "You poor chap;" or "Does your doctor know that?"

They almost seem offended to hear running compared to a heavenly experience. (Dale Ahlquist, I might mention, wonders whether the existence of runners does not call into question the very existence of God. I think his syllogism runs something like, "If people jog, how can there be a God;" to which the only Chestertonian reply is "If God had intended humans to run, he would have given us legs.")

I suppose the view of running as a potential heavenly pastime depends upon one's larger vision of heaven (though I concede for some it may fit better into a doctrine of purgatory). I do hope that for most of us heaven appears more like the celebration of a good Italian wedding than like an eternal Protestant church service. I recall an Old Testament professor of mine remarking, "When I'm gathered around the table for a good meal, and my family and friends are with me, I hope heaven is not too much better than this." He was expressing a very Hebraic sentiment about the goodness of the created order. The Church adopted this same attitude when it rejected the Gnostic and Manichean heresies that separated what was perceived as good human spirituality from sinful material being. That is why a Christian portrait of heaven can never stand as wispy and ethereal, with translucent haloed saints lounging languidly among the clouds. The scriptural depiction of heaven entails the restoration of things solid and earthly, with a new heaven and a new earth created by God, with new substantial bodies for us. Chesterton always stressed this interpretation of the life to come. *The Everlasting Man*, describes "the human instinct for a heaven that shall be as literal and almost as local as a home." The idea was fleshed out clearest in *Manalive*. Innocent Smith, the protagonist declares:

> I mean ... that if there be a house for me in heaven it will either have a green lamp-post and a hedge, or something quite as positive and personal as a green lamp-post and a hedge. I mean that God bade me love one spot and serve it, and do all things however wild in praise of it, so that this one spot might be a witness against all the infinites and sophistries, that Paradise is somewhere and not anywhere, is something and not anything.

If it is indeed true that heaven is something solidly awaiting us, then maybe heaven is worth running into.

About the Author

Robert Moore-Jumonville serves Spring Arbor University as Professor of Christian Spirituality in the Department of Theology.

He received his Bachelor of Arts in Religion and History from Seattle Pacific University, his Masters of Divinity from Princeton Theological Seminary, and earned his Ph.D. in the History of Christianity from The University of Iowa. An elder in the United Methodist Church, he has served for seventeen years as senior pastor for three churches (in Illinois, Indiana, and now Michigan). A member of West Michigan Conference since 2008, he currently pastors Pope United Methodist Church.

His publications include, *Hermeneutics of Historical Distance: Mapping the Terrain of American Biblical Criticism*, 1880-1914 (Rowan & Littlefield 2003), *Advent & Christmas Wisdom* from G. K. Chesterton, and *Lent and Easter Wisdom from G. K. Chesterton*, both with Thom Satterlee (Liguori 2007). Moore-Jumonville's bi-monthly column "Jogging With G. K". appeared for twelve years in *Gilbert Magazine*, the publication of the American Chesterton Society.

OTHER BOOKS OF INTEREST

C. S. Lewis

C. S. Lewis: Views From Wake Forest - Essays on C. S. Lewis
Michael Travers, editor

Contains sixteen scholarly presentations from the international C. S. Lewis convention in Wake Forest, NC. Walter Hooper shares his important essay "Editing C. S. Lewis," a chronicle of publishing decisions after Lewis' death in 1963.

"Scholars from a variety of disciplines address a wide range of issues. The happy result is a fresh and expansive view of an author who well deserves this kind of thoughtful attention."
Diana Pavlac Glyer, author of *The Company They Keep*

The Hidden Story of Narnia:
A Book-By-Book Guide to Lewis' Spiritual Themes
Will Vaus

A book of insightful commentary equally suited for teens or adults – Will Vaus points out connections between the *Narnia* books and spiritual/biblical themes, as well as between ideas in the *Narnia* books and C. S. Lewis' other books. Learn what Lewis himself said about the overarching and unifying thematic structure of the Narnia books. That is what this book explores; what C. S. Lewis called "the hidden story" of Narnia. Each chapter includes questions for individual use or small group discussion.

Why I Believe in Narnia:
33 Reviews and Essays on the Life and Work of C.S. Lewis
James Como

Chapters range from reviews of critical books , documentaries and movies to evaluations of Lewis' books to biographical analysis.
"A valuable, wide-ranging collection of essays by one of the best informed and most accute commentators on Lewis' work and ideas."
Peter Schakel, author of *Imagination & the Arts in C.S. Lewis*

Shadows and Chivalry:
C.S. Lewis and George MacDonald on Suffering, Evil, and Death
Jeff McInnis

Shadows and Chivalry studies the influence of George MacDonald, a nineteenth-century Scottish novelist and fantasy writer, upon one of the most influential writers of modern times, C. S. Lewis—the creator of Narnia, literary critic, and best-selling apologist. This study attempts to trace the overall affect of MacDonald's work on Lewis's thought and imagination. Without ever ceasing to be a story of one man's influence upon another, the study also serves as an exploration of each writer's thought on, and literary visions of, good and evil.

C. S. Lewis Goes to Heaven: A Reader's Guide to The Great Divorce
David G. Clark

This is the first book devoted solely to this often neglected book and the first to reveal several important secrets Lewis concealed within the story. Lewis felt his imaginary trip to Hell and Heaven was far better than his book *The Screwtape Letters*, which has become a classic. Clark has taught courses on Lewis for more than 30 years and is a New Testament and Greek scholar with a Doctor of Philosophy degree in Biblical Studies. Readers will discover the many literary and biblical influences Lewis utilized in writing his brilliant novel.

C. S. Lewis & Philosophy as a Way of Life: His Philosophical Thoughts
Adam Barkman

C. S. Lewis is rarely thought of as a "philosopher" per se despite having both studied and taught philosophy for several years at Oxford. Lewis's long journey to Christianity was essentially philosophical – passing through seven different stages. This 624 page book is an invaluable reference for C. S. Lewis scholars and fans alike

C. S. Lewis: His Literary Achievement
Colin Manlove

"This is a positively brilliant book, written with splendor, elegance, profundity and evidencing an enormous amount of learning. This is probably not a book to give a first-time reader of Lewis. But for those who are more broadly read in the Lewis corpus this book is an absolute gold mine of information. The author gives us a magnificent overview of Lewis' many writings, tracing for us thoughts and ideas which recur throughout, and at the same time telling us how each book differs from the others. I think it is not extravagant to call C. S. Lewis: His Literary Achievement a tour de force."

Robert Merchant, St. Austin Review, Book Review Editor

Mythopoeic Narnia: Memory, Metaphor, and Metamorphoses in C. S. Lewis's The Chronicles of Narnia
Salwa Khoddam

Dr. Khoddam offers a fresh approach to the *Narnia* books based on an inquiry into Lewis' readings and use of classical and Christian symbols. She explores the literary and intellectual contexts of these stories, the traditional myths and motifs, and places them in the company of the greatest Christian mythopoeic works of Western Literature. In Lewis' imagination, memory and metaphor interact to advance his purpose – a Christian metamorphosis. *Mythopoeic Narnia* opens the door for readers into the magical world of the Western imagination.

Speaking of Jack: A C. S. Lewis Discussion Guide
Will Vaus

C. S. Lewis Societies have been forming around the world since the first one started in New York City in 1969. Will Vaus has started and led three groups himself. *Speaking of Jack* is the result of Vaus' experience in leading those Lewis Societies. Included here are introductions to most of Lewis' books as well as questions designed to stimulate discussion about Lewis' life and work. These materials have been "road-tested" with real groups made up of young and old, some very familiar with Lewis and some newcomers. *Speaking of Jack* may be used in an existing book discussion group, to start a C. S. Lewis Society, or as a guide to your own exploration of Lewis' books.

George MacDonald

Diary of an Old Soul & The White Page Poems
George MacDonald and Betty Aberlin

The first edition of George MacDonald's book of daily poems included a blank page opposite each page of poems. Readers were invited to write their own reflections on the "white page." MacDonald wrote: "Let your white page be ground, my print be seed, growing to golden ears, that faith and hope may feed." Betty Aberlin responded to MacDonald's invitation with daily poems of her own.

Betty Aberlin's close readings of George MacDonald's verses and her thoughtful responses to them speak clearly of her poetic gifts and spiritual intelligence.
Luci Shaw, poet

George MacDonald: Literary Heritage and Heirs
Roderick McGillis, editor

This latest collection of 14 essays sets a new standard that will influence MacDonald studies for many more years. George MacDonald experts are increasingly evaluating his entire corpus within the nineteenth century context.

This comprehensive collection represents the best of contemporary scholarship on George MacDonald.
Rolland Hein, author of *George MacDonald: Victorian Mythmaker*

In the Near Loss of Everything: George MacDonald's Son in America
Dale Wayne Slusser

In the summer of 1887, George MacDonald's son Ronald, newly engaged to artist Louise Blandy, sailed from England to America to teach school. The next summer he returned to England to marry Louise and bring her back to America. On August 27, 1890, Louise died leaving him with an infant daughter. Ronald once described losing a beloved spouse as "the near loss of everything". Dale Wayne Slusser unfolds this poignant story with unpublished letters and photos that give readers a glimpse into the close-knit MacDonald family. Also included is Ronald's essay about his father, *George MacDonald: A Personal Note*, plus a selection from Ronald's 1922 fable, *The Laughing Elf*, about the necessity of both sorrow and joy in life.

A Novel Pulpit: Sermons From George MacDonald's Fiction
David L. Neuhouser
Each of the sermons has an introduction giving some explanation of the setting of the sermon or of the plot, if that is necessary for understanding the sermon. *"MacDonald's novels are both stimulating and thought-provoking. This collection of sermons from ten novels serve to bring out the 'freshness and brilliance' of MacDonald's message." from the author's introduction*

Behind the Back of the North Wind: Essays on George MacDonald's Classic Book
Edited and with Introduction by John Pennington and Roderick McGillis

The unique blend of fairy tale atmosphere and social realism in this novel laid the groundwork for modern fantasy literature. Sixteen essays by various authors are accompanied by an instructive introduction, extensive index,and beautiful illustrations.

Through the Year with George MacDonald: 366 Daily Readings
Rolland Hein, editor

These page-length excerpts from sermons, novels and letters are given an appropriate theme/heading and a complementary Scripture passage for daily reading. An inspiring introduction to the artistic soul and Christian vision of George MacDonald.

Poets and Poetry

Remembering Roy Campbell: The Memoirs of his Daughters, Anna and Tess
Introduction by Judith Lütge Coullie, Editor
Preface by Joseph Pearce

Anna and Teresa Campbell were the daughters of the handsome young South African poet and writer, Roy Campbell (1901-1957), and his beautiful English wife, Mary Garman. In their frank and moving memoirs, Anna and Tess recall the extraordinary, and often very difficult, lives they shared with their exceptional parents. Over 50 photos, 344 footnotes, timeline of Campbell's life, and complete index.

In the Eye of the Beholder: How to See the World Like a Romantic Poet
Louis Markos

Born out of the French Revolution and its radical faith that a nation could be shaped and altered by the dreams and visions of its people, British Romantic Poetry was founded on a belief that the objects and realities of our world, whether natural or human, are not fixed in stone but can be molded and transformed by the visionary eye of the poet. A separate bibliographical essay is provided for readers listing accessible biographies of each poet and critical studies of their work.

The Cat on the Catamaran: A Christmas Tale
John Martin

Here is a modern-day parable of a modern-day cat with modern-day attitudes. Riverboat Dan is a "cool" cat on a perpetual vacation from responsibility. He's *The Cat on the Catamaran* – sailing down the river of life. Dan keeps his guilty conscience from interfering with his fun until he runs into trouble. But will he have the courage to believe that it's never too late to change course? (For ages 10 to adult)

"Cat lovers and poetry lovers alike will enjoy this whimsical story about Riverboat Dan, a philosophical cat in search of meaning."
Regina Doman, author of *Angel in the Water*

The Half Blood Poems
Inspired by the Stories of J.K. Rowling
Christine Lowther

Like Harry Potter, Christine's poetry can soar above the tragic to discover the heroic and beautiful in such poems as "Neville, Unlikely Rebel", "For Our Wide-Armed Mothers," and "A Boy's Hands." There are 71 poems divided into seven chapters that correspond to the seven books. Fans of Harry Potter will experience once again many of the emotions they felt reading the books – emotions presented most effectively through a poet's words.

Pop Culture

To Love Another Person: A Spiritual Journey Through Les Miserables
John Morrison

The powerful story of Jean Valjean's redemption is beloved by readers and theater goers everywhere. In this companion and guide to Victor Hugo's masterpiece, author John Morrison unfolds the spiritual depth and breadth of this classic novel and broadway musical.

Through Common Things: Philosophical Reflections on Popular Culture
Adam Barkman

"Barkman presents us with an amazingly wide-ranging collection of philosophical reflections grounded in the everyday things of popular culture – past and present, eastern and western, factual and fictional. Throughout his encounters with often surprising subject-matter (the value of darkness?), he writes clearly and concisely, moving seamlessly between Aristotle and anime, Lord Buddha and Lord Voldemort.... This is an informative and entertaining book to read!"
Doug Bloomberg, Professor of Philosophy, Institute for Christian Studies

Spotlight:
A Close-up Look at the Artistry and Meaning of Stephenie Meyer's Twilight Novels
John Granger

Stephenie Meyer's *Twilight* saga has taken the world by storm. But is there more to *Twilight* than a love story for teen girls crossed with a cheesy vampire-werewolf drama? *Spotlight* reveals the literary backdrop, themes, artistry, and meaning of the four Bella Swan adventures. *Spotlight* is the perfect gift for serious *Twilight* readers.

Virtuous Worlds: The Video Gamer's Guide to Spiritual Truth
John Stanifer

Popular titles like *Halo 3* and *The Legend of Zelda: Twilight Princess* fly off shelves at a mind-blowing rate. John Stanifer, an avid gamer, shows readers specific parallels between Christian faith and the content of their favorite games. Written with wry humor (including a heckler who frequently pokes fun at the author) this book will appeal to gamers and non-gamers alike. Those unfamiliar with video games may be pleasantly surprised to find that many elements in those "virtual worlds" also qualify them as "virtuous worlds."

The Many Faces of Katniss Everdeen: Exploring the Heroine of The Hunger Games
Valerie Estelle Frankel

Katniss is the heroine who's changed the world. Like Harry Potter, she explodes across genres: She is a dystopian heroine, a warrior woman, a reality TV star, a rebellious adolescent. She's surrounded by the figures of Roman history, from Caesar and Cato to Cinna and Coriolanus Snow. She's also traveling the classic heroine's journey. As a child soldier, she faces trauma; as a growing teen, she battles through love triangles and the struggle to be good in a harsh world. This book explores all this and more, while taking a look at the series' symbolism, from food to storytelling, to show how Katniss becomes the greatest power of Panem, the girl on fire.

Memoir

Called to Serve: Life as a Firefighter-Deacon
Deacon Anthony R. Surozenski

Called to Serve is the story of one man's dream to be a firefighter. But dreams have a way of taking detours – so Tony Soruzenski became a teacher and eventually a volunteer firefighter. And when God enters the picture, Tony is faced with a choice. Will he give up firefighting to follow another call? After many years, Tony's two callings are finally united – in service as a fire chaplain at Ground Zero after the 9-11 attacks and in other ways he could not have imagined. Tony is Chief Chaplain's aid for the Massachusettes Corp of Fire Chaplains and Director for the Office of the Diaconate of the Diocese of Worchester, Massachusettes.

Biography

Sheldon Vanauken: The Man Who Received "A Severe Mercy"
Will Vaus

In this biography we discover: Vanauken the struggling student, the bon-vivant lover, the sailor who witnessed the bombing of Pearl Harbor, the seeker who returned to faith through C. S. Lewis, the beloved professor of English literature and history, the feminist and anti-war activist who participated in the March on the Pentagon, the bestselling author, and Vanauken the convert to Catholicism. What emerges is the portrait of a man relentlessly in search of beauty, love, and truth, a man who believed that, in the end, he found all three.

"This is a charming biography about a doubly charming man who wrote a triply charming book. It is a great way to meet the man behind A Severe Mercy."

Peter Kreeft, author of *Jacob's Ladder: 10 Steps to Truth*

Fiction

The Iona Conspiracy (from The Remnant Chronicles book series)
Gary Gregg

Readers find themselves on a modern adventure through ancient Celtic myth and legend as thirteen year old Jacob uncovers his destiny within "the remnant" of the Sporrai Order. As the Iona Academy comes under the control of educational reformers and ideological scientists, Jacob finds himself on a dangerous mission to the sacred Scottish island of Iona and discovers how his life is wrapped up with the fate of the long lost cover of *The Book of Kells*. From its connections to Arthurian legend to references to real-life people, places, and historical mysteries, *Iona* is an adventure that speaks to eternal truths as well as the challenges of the modern world. A young adult novel, *Iona* can be enjoyed by the entire family.

Harry Potter

The Order of Harry Potter: The Literary Skill of the Hogwarts Epic
Colin Manlove

Colin Manlove, a popular conference speaker and author of over a dozen books, has earned an international reputation as an expert on fantasy and children's literature. His book, *From Alice to Harry Potter*, is a survey of 400 English fantasy books. In *The Order of Harry Potter*, he compares and contrasts *Harry Potter* with works by "Inklings" writers J.R.R. Tolkien, C.S. Lewis and Charles Williams; he also examines Rowling's treatment of the topic of imagination; her skill in organization and the use of language; and the book's underlying motifs and themes.

Harry Potter & Imagination: The Way Between Two Worlds
Travis Prinzi

Imaginative literature places a reader between two worlds: the story world and the world of daily life, and challenges the reader to imagine and to act for a better world. Starting with discussion of Harry Potter's more important themes, *Harry Potter & Imagination* takes readers on a journey through the transformative power of those themes for both the individual and for culture by placing Rowling's series in its literary, historical, and cultural contexts.

Repotting Harry Potter: A Professor's Guide for the Serious Re-Reader
Rowling Revisited: Return Trips to Harry, Fantastic Beasts, Quidditch, & Beedle the Bard
Dr. James W. Thomas

In *Repotting Harry Potter* and his sequel book *Rowling Revisited*, Dr. James W. Thomas points out the humor, puns, foreshadowing and literary parallels in the Potter books. In *Rowling Revisted*, readers will especially find useful three extensive appendixes – "Fantastic Beasts and the Pages Where You'll Find Them," "Quidditch Through the Pages," and "The Books in the Potter Books." Dr. Thomas makes re-reading the Potter books even more rewarding and enjoyable.

Deathly Hallows Lectures:
The Hogwarts Professor Explains Harry's Final Adventure
John Granger

In *The Deathly Hallows Lectures,* John Granger reveals the finale's brilliant details, themes, and meanings. *Harry Potter* fans will be surprised by and delighted with Granger's explanations of the three dimensions of meaning in *Deathly Hallows*. Ms. Rowling has said that alchemy sets the "parameters of magic" in the series; after reading the chapter-length explanation of *Deathly Hallows* as the final stage of the alchemical Great Work, the serious reader will understand how important literary alchemy is in understanding Rowling's artistry and accomplishment.

Hog's Head Conversations: Essays on Harry Potter
Travis Prinzi, Editor

Ten fascinating essays on Harry Potter by popular Potter writers and speakers including John Granger, James W. Thomas, Colin Manlove, and Travis Prinzi.

Sociology and Harry Potter: 22 Enchanting Essays on the Wizarding World
Jenn Simms, editor

Modeled on an Introduction to Sociology textbook. this books is not simply about the series, but also used the series to facilitate reader's understanding of the discipline of sociology and a development of a sociological approach to viewing social reality. It is a case of high quality academic scholarship written in a form and on a topic accessible to non-academics. As such, it is written to appeal to Harry Potter fans and the general reading public. Contributors include professional sociologists from eight countries.

Harry Potter, Still Recruiting:
An Inner Look at Harry Potter Fandom
Valerie Frankel, editor

The Harry Potter phenomenon has created a new world: one of Quidditch in the park, lightning earrings, endless parodies, a new genre of music, and fan conferences of epic proportions. This book attempts to document everything - exploring costuming, crafting, gaming, and more, with essays and interviews straight from the multitude of creators. From children to adults, fans are delighting the world with an explosion of captivating activities and experiences, all based on Rowling's delightful series.

Christian Living

The Living Word of the Living God:
A Beginner's Guide to Reading and Understanding the Bible
Rev. Tom Furrer

This book is based on over 20 years experience of teaching the Bible to confirmation classes at Episcopal churches in Connecticut. Chapters from Genesis to Revelation.

Keys to Growth: Meditations on the Acts of the Apostles
Will Vaus

Every living thing or person requires certain ingredients in order to grow, and if a thing or person is not growing, it is dying. *The Acts of the Apostles* is a book that is all about growth. Will Vaus has been meditating and preaching on *Acts* for the past 30 years. In this volume, he offers the reader forty-one keys from the entire book of Acts to unlock spiritual growth in everyday life.

Open Before Christmas: Devotional Thoughts For The Holiday Season
Will Vaus

Author Will Vaus seeks to deepen the reader's knowledge of Advent and Christmas leading up to Epiphany. Readers are provided with devotional thoughts for each day that help them to experience this part of the Church Year perhaps in a more spiritually enriching way than ever before.

"Seasoned with inspiring, touching, and sometimes humorous illustrations .... I found his writing immediately engaging and, the more I read, the more I liked it. God has touched my heart by reading Open Before Christmas, and I believe he will touch your heart too."
    The Rev. David Beckmann, Founder of The C.S. Lewis Society of Chattanooga

CPSIA information can be obtained
at www.ICGtesting.com
Printed in the USA
BVOW08s0735010517
482771BV00001B/111/P